If Patton's *Your Path to Nonprofit Leadership* podcast is any indication, his knowledge and mastery of nonprofit culture and careers will benefit all who read this, from those who are new to the sector to seasoned managers seeking to elevate their knowledge and skills.

—ELIZABETH ABEL

Senior Vice President, CCS Fundraising
New York City, NY

Career change can be challenging, but with *Your Path to Nonprofit Leadership*, you'll have a road map to a successful transition and ongoing professional development. What an indispensable guide!

—GAIL S. BOWER

President, Bower & Co. Consulting, LLC
Philadelphia, PA

Interested in enhancing your nonprofit acumen? *Your Path to Nonprofit Leadership* does just that by creating an effective and thoughtful approach to guide you along the way. Patton uses his clear and effective style to discuss complex topics with ease.

—ADAM A. COOK, CFRE

Chief Development Officer, Mercy Health Foundation
Chesterfield, MO

Your Path to Nonprofit Leadership is a benefit to all who are in, or who want to join, the nonprofit sector. I worked directly for Patton at UNCW and was able to learn from him every day—this book will now provide countless others that same opportunity to hear his wisdom and guidance.

—CHRIS DELISIO, MBA, CFRE

VP for Institutional Advancement, Florida Atlantic University
Boca Raton, FL

Your Path to Nonprofit Leadership is an invaluable guide for anyone who aspires to nonprofit leadership. Patton not only identifies each of the skills, assets, and experiences aspiring leaders need to develop, he takes the reader, step by simple step, through the entire self-development process. Chapter 3 alone, on the ten essential skills and experiences, is worth the cover price a hundred times over.

—MARTYN DRAKE

Author, The Commercial Charity
Binley Drake Consulting Ltd
Nottinghamshire, England, United Kingdom

What makes Patton's teaching so powerful is that he's built a career from the ground up, having served in all key aspects of nonprofit work as volunteer, staff member, board member, and consultant. This book should be on your list of great resources for guidance and reflection.

—KEITH L. FISHBURNE

President and CEO, Special Olympics North Carolina
Morrisville, NC

Patton is the Wayne Gretzky of philanthropy. He knows where the puck has been, but more importantly, he knows where it's going. And he willingly shares his expertise so that my organization can get in the game with confidence and put points on the board.

—KEN D. FUQUAY
CEO, LIFESPAN Services
Charlotte, NC

Patton's years of experience in the nonprofit sector have given him incredible insights into best practices and leadership development. His personal knowledge and podcast interviews with nonprofit leaders from around the world make this book an essential part of your professional development plan.

—JENNIFER P. GARNER, MA
Executive Director of Development, University of Denver
Denver, CO

Your Path to Nonprofit Leadership is a must-read for any leader who is focused on their legacy. Patton channels his experience and down-to-earth approach to inspire his readers to action. From being introspective to gaining perspective to being effective, this book covers it all on the nonprofit leadership journey.

—SAMARA HAKIM, JD
Founder, CulturGrit
San Diego, CA

Patton's refreshing take on the nonprofit leadership journey bridges skill-building and self-reliance with community support. Developing a personal case and mobilizing our own board gives all of us, in any role, the capabilities and the resilience to truly lead from the inside, out—to walk the path and build it at the same time.

—JENNIFER HARRIS, MA

Founder, JH Collective, Inc.
San Diego, CA

In the world of nonprofits, Patton is like one of those experienced football coaches who have seen it all: every offensive set, every defensive formation. He's always ten steps ahead of the opponent. His new book crystallizes the lessons he's been teaching and coaching on nonprofit leadership throughout his career.

—CLAY HODGES, JD

Partner, Harris, Sarratt, & Hodges, LLP
Raleigh, NC

The nonprofit sector may at first let you down, then become messier than you could have imagined, and in the end, still prove to be the most rewarding career possible. If anyone is qualified to provide guidance and encouragement for those who dare to venture down the nonprofit path, it's Patton.

—JASON LEWIS

Founder, Responsive Fundraising
Host, The Fundraising Talent Podcast
York County, PA

Patton has worked in the nonprofit field for decades with leaders at every stage. Personally, I have benefitted from his career advice to build a personal board of directors, a topic in this book. I'm excited for people interested in nonprofit leadership to have a resource from Patton that clearly marks the way to success.

—SALLY LOFTIS, MSOD
Managing Director, Loftis Partners
Crossnore, NC

Your Path to Nonprofit Leadership is more than tips, techniques, and tactics. Patton has taken the painstaking effort to assemble expert perspectives from a wide array of charitable sector professionals. This practical resource is a solid addition to the toolkit of any nonprofit professional, regardless of where they are in the leadership journey.

—BEN MOHLER, MA, CFRE, ACFRE
CEO and Principal Consultant, GivingThree, LLC
Richmond, KY

Patton's enthusiasm for—and deep knowledge of—the nonprofit world has always impressed me. *Your Path to Nonprofit Leadership* will be a powerful guide for any nonprofit leader hoping to excel in the charitable sector.

—MIKE SMITH
Founder, BIGiDEASPORTS
Barcelona, Spain

As a two-time guest on Patton's weekly *Your Path to Nonprofit Leadership* podcast, I've marveled at his insightful observations about the current state of the nonprofit sector. I believe this book will be an essential resource for the growth of current and aspiring nonprofit leaders.

—JIM TAYLOR
Vice President of Leadership Initiatives, BoardSource
Washington, DC

Patton has worked in the nonprofit field for decades with leaders at every stage. Personally, I have benefitted from his career advice to build a personal board of directors, a topic in this book. I'm excited for people interested in nonprofit leadership to have a resource from Patton that clearly marks the way to success.

—SALLY LOFTIS, MSOD
Managing Director, Loftis Partners
Crossnore, NC

Your Path to Nonprofit Leadership is more than tips, techniques, and tactics. Patton has taken the painstaking effort to assemble expert perspectives from a wide array of charitable sector professionals. This practical resource is a solid addition to the toolkit of any nonprofit professional, regardless of where they are in the leadership journey.

—BEN MOHLER, MA, CFRE, ACFRE
CEO and Principal Consultant, GivingThree, LLC
Richmond, KY

Patton's enthusiasm for—and deep knowledge of—the nonprofit world has always impressed me. *Your Path to Nonprofit Leadership* will be a powerful guide for any nonprofit leader hoping to excel in the charitable sector.

—MIKE SMITH
Founder, BIGiDEASPORTS
Barcelona, Spain

As a two-time guest on Patton's weekly *Your Path to Nonprofit Leadership* podcast, I've marveled at his insightful observations about the current state of the nonprofit sector. I believe this book will be an essential resource for the growth of current and aspiring nonprofit leaders.

—JIM TAYLOR
Vice President of Leadership Initiatives, BoardSource
Washington, DC

YOUR PATH TO

Nonprofit
Leadership

Dr. Patton McDowell, MBA, CFRE

YOUR PATH TO
Nonprofit
Leadership

SEVEN KEYS TO ADVANCING YOUR CAREER
IN THE PHILANTHROPIC SECTOR

Published by Advantage, Charleston, South Carolina.
Member of Advantage Media Group.

ADVANTAGE is a registered trademark, and the Advantage colophon is a trademark of Advantage Media Group, Inc.

Printed in the United States of America.

10 9 8 7 6 5 4 3 2 1

ISBN: 978-1-64225-197-5
LCCN: 2021920504

This publication is designed to provide accurate and authoritative information in regard to the subject matter covered. It is sold with the understanding that the publisher is not engaged in rendering legal, accounting, or other professional services. If legal advice or other expert assistance is required, the services of a competent professional person should be sought.

 Advantage Media Group is proud to be a part of the Tree Neutral® program. Tree Neutral offsets the number of trees consumed in the production and printing of this book by taking proactive steps such as planting trees in direct proportion to the number of trees used to print books. To learn more about Tree Neutral, please visit **www.treeneutral.com**.

Advantage Media Group is a publisher of business, self-improvement, and professional development books and online learning. We help entrepreneurs, business leaders, and professionals share their Stories, Passion, and Knowledge to help others Learn & Grow. Do you have a manuscript or book idea that you would like us to consider for publishing? Please visit **advantagefamily.com**.

Dr. Patton McDowell, MBA, CFRE

YOUR PATH TO
Nonprofit
Leadership

SEVEN KEYS TO ADVANCING YOUR CAREER
IN THE PHILANTHROPIC SECTOR

Published by Advantage, Charleston, South Carolina.
Member of Advantage Media Group.

ADVANTAGE is a registered trademark, and the Advantage colophon is a trademark of Advantage Media Group, Inc.

Printed in the United States of America.

10 9 8 7 6 5 4 3 2 1

ISBN: 978-1-64225-197-5
LCCN: 2021920504

This publication is designed to provide accurate and authoritative information in regard to the subject matter covered. It is sold with the understanding that the publisher is not engaged in rendering legal, accounting, or other professional services. If legal advice or other expert assistance is required, the services of a competent professional person should be sought.

 Advantage Media Group is proud to be a part of the Tree Neutral® program. Tree Neutral offsets the number of trees consumed in the production and printing of this book by taking proactive steps such as planting trees in direct proportion to the number of trees used to print books. To learn more about Tree Neutral, please visit **www.treeneutral.com**.

Advantage Media Group is a publisher of business, self-improvement, and professional development books and online learning. We help entrepreneurs, business leaders, and professionals share their Stories, Passion, and Knowledge to help others Learn & Grow. Do you have a manuscript or book idea that you would like us to consider for publishing? Please visit **advantagefamily.com**.

To Cindy, who inspired my path to nonprofit leadership.

CONTENTS

CONTENTS

ACKNOWLEDGMENTS

This book would not be possible without the experience I've gained through working with nearly 250 nonprofit organizations and their fantastic staff and board leaders. I've also been able to learn many leadership lessons as a result of being part of outstanding organizations such as the Special Olympics International and working with people like its founder, Eunice Kennedy Shriver; Dave Lenox, the executive director of the Special Olympics North Carolina; Jim Leutze, chancellor at UNC Wilmington; and Pamela Davies, president of Queens University of Charlotte. I'm also especially grateful for the many dedicated colleagues who have worked with me at PMA Consulting since its founding in 2009, including our current team of Jean Bock, Katelynn Bruno, Cindy Clark, Penny Hawkins, Charmain Lewis, Lauren McDowell, Cindy Teddy, Lea Williams, and Ashlee Yochim.

A book project like this doesn't happen without the support of friends and family who provide guidance, encouragement, and a kick in the pants when necessary. For me, it all starts with my mom and dad, Pat and Dianne McDowell, who instilled a focus on education, community service, and lifelong learning in my siblings, Kelly, Beth, Bryan, and me. My wife, Cindy, and I are fortunate to have three wonderful kids, Katie, Lauren, and Parker, whose personal and professional ambitions include the nonprofit community. My mother-in-law, Linda Sue Pinkston, provides a constant source of energy and encouragement for my work, my writing, and the podcast.

In addition to the immediate family support, I'm grateful for the Outer Banks hospitality from my Uncle Rufus and Aunt Roxie Pritchard, who provided the quiet getaway I needed to get this done, as well as a similar writing retreat from my in-laws George and Alice Pinkston. I'm fortunate to have a talented group of friends and mentors who have helped me along the way, especially as I was developing the nonprofit leadership concepts that evolved into PMA Consulting: Michael and Kim Barclift, Peter and Cathy Browning, Cutter and Greta Davis, Chris and Stephani Delisio, Jay and Kim Dowd, Clay and Kelly Hodges, Ricky May, Page and Cathy Singletary, and Will Sparks. Thanks to the great team at Advantage|ForbesBooks, including Laura Rashley, Laura Grinstead, and Ann Aubrey Hansen, who helped shape the path to be an accessible guide to nonprofit leadership. Special thanks to my colleagues Lea Williams and Jean Bock, who brought strategic focus to this book while simultaneously juggling multiple projects for the firm.

INTRODUCTION

E veryone has a nonprofit cause they support. Perhaps it is the after-school program that first introduced you to youth sports and now provides an opportunity to serve as a volunteer coach. Maybe it is the children's museum that first sparked your interest in nature that continues through your weekend explorations of state and national parks. Or, sadly, maybe the loss of a loved one to cancer, Alzheimer's, or heart disease fuels your devotion to a nonprofit organization.

While everyone may have a cause, for most individuals, the extent of their involvement extends no further than being a volunteer, donor, or champion. Your interest in this book, however, suggests that your interest in a nonprofit cause—or several causes—is more than that. Maybe you are feeling compelled toward action and inspired to pursue nonprofit leadership in a thoughtful and serious manner. If that is the case, this book is for you.

There is certainly more than one path to nonprofit leadership. You may be in the midst of a university program that has introduced you to nonprofit work, and the career possibilities intrigue you. You may be ten years into a for-profit job and realize it is not what you thought it would be. Or you may already be working in the nonprofit sector but are now realizing that leading an organization is your ultimate goal.

Regardless of where you are on the nonprofit path, this book is designed to help you identify your leadership goal and create a detailed plan to get you there. To help you create the plan, I will address some of the basic questions that may be on your mind right now:

- What does nonprofit leadership look like?

- How do I position myself for a leadership role?

- What should I do first?

I have spent my entire thirty-year career helping individuals raise funds for causes they are passionate about and effectively lead their nonprofit organizations. In 2009, I founded Patton McDowell & Associates ("PMA"); since then, I have worked with the leaders of almost 250 nonprofit organizations in every sector, including education, healthcare, arts and culture, and human services. Prior to my work as a coach and consultant, I spent a decade in higher education, including five years as vice president for university advancement at Queens University of Charlotte and five years as vice chancellor for university advancement at UNC Wilmington, where I was the youngest vice chancellor in the UNC system.

Before going to Wilmington, I served as program director for Special Olympics North Carolina in Raleigh for seven years, following two years with Special Olympics International in Washington, DC. My work for Special Olympics included the creation of a unique volunteer training system called Sport Development Teams, still in use today worldwide.

While my path may sound linear, I can assure you it has been unconventional, which I will elaborate on in chapter 1, "Why Nonprofits?" I have asked myself the same questions you have on your

INTRODUCTION

E veryone has a nonprofit cause they support. Perhaps it is the after-school program that first introduced you to youth sports and now provides an opportunity to serve as a volunteer coach. Maybe it is the children's museum that first sparked your interest in nature that continues through your weekend explorations of state and national parks. Or, sadly, maybe the loss of a loved one to cancer, Alzheimer's, or heart disease fuels your devotion to a nonprofit organization.

While everyone may have a cause, for most individuals, the extent of their involvement extends no further than being a volunteer, donor, or champion. Your interest in this book, however, suggests that your interest in a nonprofit cause—or several causes—is more than that. Maybe you are feeling compelled toward action and inspired to pursue nonprofit leadership in a thoughtful and serious manner. If that is the case, this book is for you.

There is certainly more than one path to nonprofit leadership. You may be in the midst of a university program that has introduced you to nonprofit work, and the career possibilities intrigue you. You may be ten years into a for-profit job and realize it is not what you thought it would be. Or you may already be working in the nonprofit sector but are now realizing that leading an organization is your ultimate goal.

Regardless of where you are on the nonprofit path, this book is designed to help you identify your leadership goal and create a detailed plan to get you there. To help you create the plan, I will address some of the basic questions that may be on your mind right now:

- What does nonprofit leadership look like?

- How do I position myself for a leadership role?

- What should I do first?

I have spent my entire thirty-year career helping individuals raise funds for causes they are passionate about and effectively lead their nonprofit organizations. In 2009, I founded Patton McDowell & Associates ("PMA"); since then, I have worked with the leaders of almost 250 nonprofit organizations in every sector, including education, healthcare, arts and culture, and human services. Prior to my work as a coach and consultant, I spent a decade in higher education, including five years as vice president for university advancement at Queens University of Charlotte and five years as vice chancellor for university advancement at UNC Wilmington, where I was the youngest vice chancellor in the UNC system.

Before going to Wilmington, I served as program director for Special Olympics North Carolina in Raleigh for seven years, following two years with Special Olympics International in Washington, DC. My work for Special Olympics included the creation of a unique volunteer training system called Sport Development Teams, still in use today worldwide.

While my path may sound linear, I can assure you it has been unconventional, which I will elaborate on in chapter 1, "Why Nonprofits?" I have asked myself the same questions you have on your mind right now and learned many lessons along the way from which I hope you will benefit.

This book is designed to answer these fundamental questions and provide the practical tools and guidance you need to put together a personal strategic plan that will acknowledge where you are on your professional journey, better define your goal, and help you to chart a course to nonprofit leadership.

This book will help you to accomplish that through seven distinct steps that comprise your path to nonprofit leadership:

1. Sharpen your vision

2. Map your course

3. Get in shape

4. Curate knowledge

5. Express yourself

6. Build community

7. Practice leadership

Each of these steps will be defined by exactly how they support nonprofit leadership, and you will learn what you need to do to strengthen your skills and gain experiences to ensure leadership success. You will be presented with specific and attainable actions to work on *right now* to create a map illustrating your path to nonprofit leadership. Your map will include distinct steps to guide your long-term vision over the next five to ten years, your strategic goals in the next three to five years, and your tactical activities in the next year (and even in the next ninety days).

Of course, nonprofit leadership is not easy, and it is not for everyone. This book will offer a clear path but will require a commitment of time and energy and the discipline to make progress on each of the Seven Steps outlined using the tools and resources I provide. For some, this book may inform—and change—your career path and suggest that a full-time nonprofit leadership role is not the ultimate goal. But the leadership elements on the path can still provide guidance to serve as a more effective volunteer or board member for a cause most meaningful to you.

If nonprofit leadership is truly your goal, then you are in the right place, and this book will not only help you sharpen your skills and expand your opportunities in the field, but it will also help you guide others on the path. The strongest nonprofits embrace leadership development throughout the organization, and by strengthening your leadership on the path, you will also be a more effective guide for your staff, your board, and your volunteers.

Is this a good time to consider nonprofit leadership? No profession has absolute certainty as a long-term career path, and like every other, the nonprofit sector is impacted by global trends in technology, economic conditions, and market forces that affect job availability and turnover. A survey by the *Chronicle of Philanthropy*[1] suggests that half of the nonprofit fundraisers who responded to their poll planned to leave their current position within a year, and one-third planned to leave the field entirely in the next three years. The *Chronicle*'s study is indicative of both the challenges and the opportunities inherent in nonprofit leadership. Given the transition of so many current nonprofit professionals, opportunities abound, but the volume of turnover in the profession suggests that aspiring leaders should be quite clear about what you are looking for and

---

1   Heather Joslyn, "51% of Fundraisers Plan to Leave Their Jobs by 2021, Says New Survey," *Chronicle of Philanthropy*, August 6, 2019, www.philanthropy.com/article/51-of-fundraisers-plan-to-leave-their-jobs-by-2021-says-new-survey/.

what organizational characteristics must be in place to ensure that your path takes you to the right destination.

If you are willing to roll up your sleeves and dive into this pursuit of nonprofit leadership, then I am eager to help you. The need for effective leadership in the nonprofit sector is only increasing: the *2019 Nonprofit Employment Report*[2] from the Johns Hopkins Nonprofit Economic Data Project (NED) shows nonprofits added nearly four times the jobs their for-profit counterparts did in the decade following the 2008 economic recession. Currently, nonprofit employees make up the third-largest workforce among US industries.

Armed with the tools in this book, you will be well positioned to advance your leadership at your current nonprofit organization, at your next nonprofit organization, or at your first nonprofit organization.

Let's begin.

---

2   Lester M. Salamon and Chelsea L. Newhouse, *The 2019 Nonprofit Employment Report*, Nonprofit Economic Data Bulletin no. 47 (Baltimore: Johns Hopkins Center for Civil Society Studies, January 2019). Available at ccss.jhu.edu.

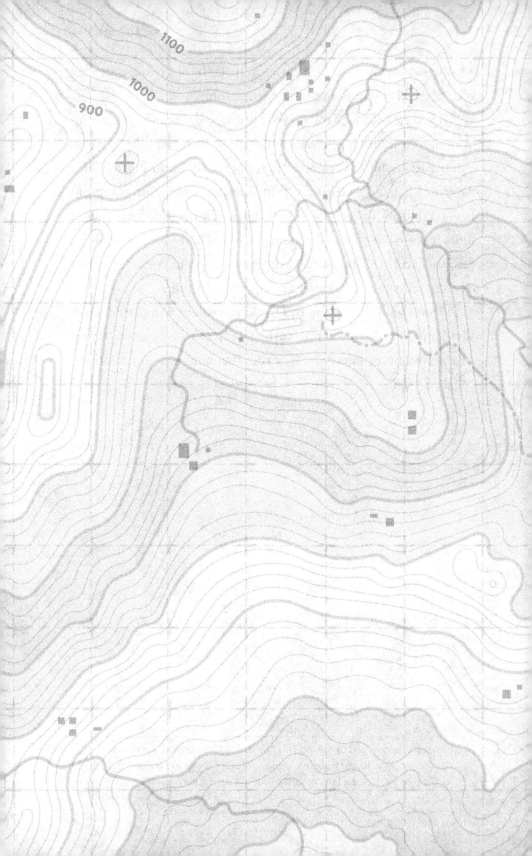

CHAPTER 1

Why Nonprofits?

My path to nonprofit leadership was unconventional and did not start with an inspirational moment or because of a cause I supported as a child. I wanted to be a high school English teacher and basketball coach, perhaps hoping to exorcise my demons as a student and unfulfilled athlete in high school. While I trudged through my college years at UNC Chapel Hill, I was fortunate to have a series of summer internship opportunities as a result of being a Morehead Scholar. The final summer session was an opportunity to serve as an intern at Special Olympics International (SOI), a global movement providing year-round competition and training for individuals with intellectual disabilities. I had enjoyed volunteering for the organization while in high school, but my motivation for that summer was more about having fun in the nation's capital while I figured out what to do with the rest of my life.

Fortunately for me, I was quickly immersed in a fascinating and complex global nonprofit, still actively managed at the time by its founder, Eunice Kennedy Shriver. Up to that point, I saw nonprofit work as a temporary career step at best, something you would do while you looked for a "real" job. Little did I know, Special Olympics proved to be every bit a real job, with career-defining opportunities on the horizon as well as a competitive salary. I wasn't going to get rich, but I wasn't going to have to get a second job either.

Mrs. Shriver started the organization in her Maryland backyard as a tribute to her sister Rosemary and to provide her an opportunity to participate in sports and activities just like everyone else, despite her disability. What began as a neighborhood activity grew into a global movement, and Mrs. Shriver built a complex international organization that featured thirty different Olympic-style sports and ninety-five participating countries by the time I arrived in 1988.

Being surrounded by talented individuals who were passionate about the Special Olympics' cause was both motivational and instructive for me. While the public-facing games and competitions illustrated the program, I was fortunate to see the critical behind-the-scenes elements, such as volunteer training and curriculum development, board and staff interactions and partnerships, communication and marketing, and individual and corporate philanthropy. From Mrs. Shriver directly, I learned the importance of a consistent articulation of mission and the equally vital importance of clarity of vision. *Where you are going* as an organization is just as important as what you are accomplishing right now.

My path to nonprofit leadership was opening up right before my eyes. I quickly realized the sector had opportunities that appealed to the mission-fulfilling elements I was seeking from coaching and teaching but also offered the professional rigor and business acumen of the for-profit world. Working for the competition and training department at SOI gave me invaluable opportunities to see nonprofit organizations both within the United States as well as in the Caribbean, Canada, and New Zealand. I tried to absorb the administration of the competition and training from the perspective of the international headquarters, but also appreciate the program from the perspective of the athletes, coaches, and families who made the program happen.

Where you are going as an organization is just as important as what you are accomplishing right now.

I was hooked. For the next seven years, I followed this nonprofit path by building on the education I had received at SOI by taking on the program director role for Special Olympics North Carolina (SONC). My destination on the path was not clear, but I knew I was getting great experience, and I wanted to build on it so that I could have opportunities for senior leadership. Some of the steps that ultimately became the core tenets of *Your Path to Nonprofit Leadership* were coming into focus at the time. I was beginning to curate knowledge, as the Seven Steps on *Your Path to Nonprofit Leadership* and the related *Five Keys to Nonprofit Excellence* were becoming clear as being crucial to my professional success. We will get into the specifics of these later on in the book, but let me now introduce you to those Seven Steps and Five Keys.

The Seven Steps on Your Path to Nonprofit Leadership

I am convinced—based on research I did for my doctoral degree and after more than thirty years of experience—that following this seven-step methodology is critical for those looking to advance successfully into leadership roles in the nonprofit sector. Each of the subsequent chapters of this book will focus on a step; I explain the concept (i.e., "the why"), discuss specific tools, and also provide additional resources for all Seven Steps:

1. Sharpen your vision

2. Map your course

3. Get in shape

4. Curate knowledge

5. Express yourself

6. Build community

7. Practice leadership

The Five Keys to Nonprofit Excellence

My work with more than 250 unique nonprofits has also confirmed that outstanding organizations focus on these Five Key objectives. You will find these keys mentioned throughout the book; I discuss them in conjunction with the Seven Steps as they are quite complementary to the steps individual leaders must follow:

1. Develop clarity of vision

2. Focus on developing staff and board talent

3. Build internal and external partnerships

4. Commit to all five phases of the fundraising cycle

5. Innovate but also measure with accountability

As my Special Olympics experience continued to add value to my résumé, the concept of a personal strategic plan began to take

shape. Utilizing the same techniques that we will explore in this book, I began to *sharpen my vision* and map out my career path, utilizing techniques such as a personal SWOT (strengths, weaknesses, opportunities, and threats) analysis, as well as short-, medium-, and long-range time horizons to build out the plan. My SWOT analysis made it clear that to develop opportunities for senior nonprofit leadership, I would need to be proficient and experienced in the art and science of fundraising, and this principle holds true for anyone exploring nonprofit leadership. Philanthropy is an integral part of the charitable sector and is also a critical component that leaders must understand to ensure the viability of their nonprofit businesses.

After seven years managing the programs for SONC, I began to explore opportunities that would allow me to sharpen my skills in fund development. A friend mentioned an opportunity available at the University of North Carolina Wilmington (UNCW) to lead their athletic fundraising efforts. The opportunity allowed me to continue my interest in sports management and utilize my program development skills as well. I also quickly realized that fundraising was very much a team sport. I knew my success would hinge upon the organization and motivation of the athletic booster club at UNCW, known as the Seahawk Club. Depending on how one looked at it, the challenge

> Philanthropy is an integral part of the charitable sector and is also a critical component that leaders must understand to ensure the viability of their nonprofit businesses.

or opportunity at UNCW was the community's recovery from two recent hurricanes in 1996, Bertha and Fran, and the region was still in a rebuilding mode, both literally and figuratively.

For me, it was a situation that could only get better, and it became a theme of my career exploration and my desire to coach nonprofit leaders from that moment forward. I knew I gravitated to an organization that had each of the Five Keys at its core, and UNCW had all of these characteristics and a clarity of vision from its dynamic chancellor, Jim Leutze. He was willing to take a chance on me despite my lack of specific experience in higher education or athletic fundraising, perhaps for the same reasons I was considering the opportunity: he wanted a fresh start, something different, and there was nowhere to go but up.

UNCW proved to be a fantastic five years of growth, both professionally and for our family as well. As our second and third children were born in Wilmington, the Seahawk Club began to thrive thanks to a cohort of enthusiastic volunteers who came together to rebuild the community spirit and accelerate the fundraising that fueled the athletic program at the university. For me, it was especially gratifying to see my skills and experiences translating to a different organizational setting. I became more sensitive to the structural elements that are critical to nonprofit leadership, something we will talk about in depth later on:

- Personal organization and productivity

- Effective communication in both directions: To my bosses and to those who reported to me

- Strategic networking: Intellectual cultivation of a network and ultimately a "personal board of directors"

I was thriving in this new environment, and after a year, I saw my professional path moving toward athletic administration, perhaps as a college athletic director. However, Chancellor Leutze made a change on his senior team with the departure of the most senior fundraiser on campus, the vice chancellor of university advancement. In a surprising move, he asked me to serve as the interim vice chancellor, elevating me to the cabinet of UNCW's administrative team and making me the youngest vice chancellor in the UNC system. I was honored to be chosen but assumed this would be a temporary yet invaluable experience. Despite my early requests of the chancellor to return to the athletic department, I soon realized that the vice chancellor role provided a unique and fascinating leadership challenge and that I enjoyed the variety of helping raise funds for the School of Nursing one day and the School of Business the next. I still had the opportunity to lead the fundraising efforts for the athletic department but was more conscious of developing the talent necessary to implement individual units' strategies as well as to ensure that they coordinated effectively across the relatively small Wilmington community. After a few months in the interim role, the chancellor named me the permanent vice chancellor, and my vision of nonprofit leadership expanded again.

Leadership lessons were coming to me at a rapid pace, and I tried to absorb as much as I could as an internal team leader, as well as maintain the external relationships that were critical for both me and for the university. I was especially grateful that Chancellor Leutze was highly supportive of the professional development opportunities available to me and my team and that he also encouraged me to get involved in the community through other nonprofits. This certainly demonstrated the university's commitment to the community but also gave me a taste of consulting, as I was asked to help with strategic planning and fundraising initiatives for various organizations outside of the university. I was also in a position to hire and work with other consultants on our campus and explore their career paths and consulting philosophies. Their input and my ongoing community involvement helped sharpen my vision for a yet-undetermined nonprofit consulting practice.

As Chancellor Leutze neared retirement, I contemplated my next career move, but just as the opportunity in Wilmington appeared as the result of my personal and professional network, so, too, did the next opportunity that led me to my tenure at Queens University of Charlotte. A consultant who had worked with me at UNCW mentioned that a dynamic new president had been named at Queens and that the university also had banking icon Hugh McColl as its board chair. I was intrigued but not really compelled by the prospect of moving the family from a university and community that we had grown to love. However, I quickly learned of the charismatic leadership that McColl used to build Bank of America, as well as the strategic vision Pamela Davies was bringing to the university as its next president.

While the prospect of leaving Wilmington was difficult to imagine, it remained within the "vision framework" that I continue to use in advising others when they are contemplating a career move:

- Does it fit within the professional role, sector, and geography defined by my vision framework?

- Is it a good opportunity for me personally as well as for my family?

- Does it offer educational and professional development opportunities?

- Does it allow for financial growth and networking potential?

Despite the inherent challenges of moving—especially with young kids—my wife, Cindy, and I decided that the opportunity at Queens did meet the criteria established through our vision framework, and Charlotte represented a new level of opportunity that would benefit our family.

President Davies proved to be an outstanding leader for the university and also a fantastic mentor for me personally. As the first external hire to join her leadership team, I was able to witness her approach to strategic planning for the institution, a topic she was well suited to manage, given her PhD in competitive strategy. It was during that period I began to assess my professional skills and experiences and implement many of the rituals and planning routines that have carried me to this day, including an annual personal planning retreat, a personal SWOT analysis, a personal board of directors, and a more extensive use of a journaling practice.

President Davies was also integral in encouraging me to enhance my academic credentials through a master's degree. As the lead fundraiser balancing the demands of work and a young family, I did not see any window of opportunity to pursue such an endeavor. However, her persistent encouragement, as well as Cindy's reinforcement from home, made the pursuit of an MBA more realistic. Of course, where else could I work that literally provided graduate education only two buildings from my office? Fortunately for me, a fantastic graduate school experience awaited me at Queens's own McColl School of Business, and I was able to address some of the professional weaknesses that I felt I needed to address to achieve my goal to be a senior leader in the nonprofit world. My self-analysis of key professional competencies (which led to the creation of the Ten Essential Skills and Experiences that are detailed in this book) confirmed that I learned some of the business skills and financial acumen necessary to manage a business of any kind. As an English education major, I found the prospect of accounting and finance classes was nothing short of terrifying. Fortunately for me, the MBA program provided both the content and the practical application that allowed me to benefit from the learning and also discover that I enjoyed aspects of graduate education I thought would be completely foreign to myself as a liberal arts major.

Learning the fundamentals of business provided a fascinating new lens through which I could strategically evaluate nonprofit organizations and also deepened my conviction to explore nonprofit consulting and ultimately have my own practice. Bolstered by my MBA and continuing work in the community with various nonprofits, I was ripe for an offer to join a local nonprofit consulting firm following five years at Queens. While the firm I joined in 2008 was not what I expected and proved to be a professional mistake, the experience proved I was skilled at the nuances of coaching and consulting, and I knew that I had arrived at a place where I could thrive.

Of course, 2008 was an incredibly challenging time for any type of organization, whether it be for-profit or nonprofit, as the result of the economic recession that challenged the national economy. It was also an uncertain time to contemplate starting a business, but that is exactly what I decided to do. My brief tenure with another firm taught me some valuable lessons, and I was determined to apply what I learned from that experience—and my professional journey to date—and apply it to the formation of my consulting practice, Patton McDowell & Associates. This was a pivotal moment in my career, and it allowed me to put into practice many of the strategic tools that have continued to benefit me and those I have worked with ever since.

Making a Strategic Review of My Network

I quickly learned that your contact list (or Rolodex, for those over the age of forty!) is more valuable than you think. I went back through my career journey in a chronological fashion and immediately found that

I had already encountered professional contacts at every step along the way. The fact remains that nearly everyone "has a cause," and I was looking for individuals who worked as staff or board members for nonprofit organizations. I was not sure what to expect at first, but my list grew quickly as I moved back through time: friends from my hometown and connections through my family, contacts from my undergraduate days at UNC Chapel Hill, connections from Special Olympics International and Special Olympics NC, community leaders and trustees associated with UNCW, and the broader network I had developed in higher education and continued through the many connections I had made in Charlotte and at Queens. After close friends and family offered their connections, too, my list grew exponentially, and I began my strategic "tour" of more than fifty personal meetings and invaluable phone conversations.

The Development of a Personal Case for Support

As good fundraisers know, a critical tool necessary for requesting philanthropic support is the "case for support"—a compelling message that explains the rationale behind the request. I was convinced that my conversations with this talented group of networking connections would be more valuable for me—and more engaging for them—if I had a conversational framework that was more than simply, "I'm trying to start a business—can you help?" In each case, I did three things:

- I did my homework. With what nonprofit organizations were they associated?

- I asked them to share the most rewarding and challenging aspects of their nonprofit experience.

- I presented the framework for what became the Five Keys and asked them if any of the five resonated for their organization.

I am convinced that this organized approach made these meetings comfortable for my contacts because it focused the conversation on the causes most meaningful to them and did not put them in the awkward position of being solicited for business. Of course, their nonprofit stories confirmed in my mind the challenges that nonprofit leaders were facing and sharpened my focus regarding what type of consulting support would be most helpful. I was careful not to push too hard for "leads" for immediate business other than to offer pro bono consulting or group facilitation. Fortunately, this subtle approach did lead to increasingly viable prospects, and the dozens of handwritten notes with my new business card enclosed led to actual paying clients. Patton McDowell & Associates was off and running thanks to my friend Cutter Davis and his recommendation, which led to a board retreat for the American Red Cross chapter in western North Carolina.

The Development of a Personal Board of Directors

As a freshly minted MBA graduate, I knew the basics of starting a small business, but I also knew that I had a lot to learn and that I would benefit from counsel myself. Inspired by Keith Ferrazzi's "personal board" concept, I began to formulate a target list for a potential board, which corresponded nicely with my existing six-month outreach to nearly seventy-five networking contacts. As described in more detail later in this book, I considered the characteristics of the board that would be most helpful to build a nonprofit consulting practice. First,

I needed to make sure the operations of a small business were secure, and I immediately identified an attorney friend and another who was an accountant. I then identified two retired business leaders who could speak to the journey of starting and expanding a business. Finally, I identified three other contacts who were subject-matter experts: a consultant, a nonprofit CEO, and a nonprofit board chair. These seven individuals, while never formally assembling at a classic board room table, provided the collective wisdom and tactical advice that helped launch the firm and continue to guide me to this day.

I am grateful that these three career-building tactics paid off. The effort to strategically network, to craft a personal case for support, and to build a personal board of directors are all tools that are part of your path to nonprofit leadership. After ramping up my practice in 2009, what I now call PMA Consulting has worked with nearly 250 nonprofits and has helped to guide countless nonprofit staff and board leaders. While I was thrilled to be leading a consulting practice focused on vital community missions in every nonprofit sector, I knew that just as I was coaching individuals to be lifelong learners, I was also following my own advice and was leading a firm that was first and foremost a learning organization. How did I do these things? Three ways:

- Realizing the value of continuing education through my MBA experience, I continued to evaluate opportunities for academic enrichment and certification that would test my thinking through new content and rigor. While I felt that my direct fundraising experience from leading two university teams—as well as counseling several dozen nonprofit campaigns—was invaluable to me as a fundraiser, the badge of honor necessary was the Certified Fundraising Executive (CFRE) recognition, and I set my sights on obtaining (and ultimately renewing twice) the CFRE.

- I also knew that the art and science of presentation and training was something I could always learn more about, and AFP International's Master Trainer training and coursework would be a valuable test of my existing skills as well as a great opportunity to enhance my understanding of adult education techniques and methodologies.

- Finally, I continue to build on a fundamental principle highlighted on the path, which is to seek expertise through *content*, such as the CFRE, and through *experience*, such as that provided by the AFP Master Trainer program.

The ultimate combination of content and practical experience proved to be a doctoral program through the University of Southern California. This unique program of engaging online courses combined with live sessions with my cohort proved to be everything I hoped it would be in terms of cutting-edge content from the fields of organizational change and leadership, as well as the ability to apply what I was learning to the nonprofit organization with which I was working. To top it all off, my dissertation allowed me to study the successes of board members in fundraising after one nonprofit has merged with another. This qualitative research allowed me to explore national trends around nonprofit mergers over the last decade and has helped me to advise organizations now that have merged with another or are pondering the possibility.

While I am proud of these achievements along my recent professional journey, what is more important is what they represent in terms of a commitment to lifelong learning and a systematic approach to the analysis of skills, content, and experience. I hope my journey gives you some ideas that you can apply to your professional development plan, regardless of where you are on your leadership journey. I will continue to use relevant stories from my journey but also bring in leadership stories from dynamic leaders in the nonprofit community, many of whom I have had the chance to interview through my podcast, *Your Path to Nonprofit Leadership*. By combining actual leadership advice with research-based content, I hope you will find the Seven Steps along the path outlined in this book to be a practical and motivating system to help you move to your desired leadership position in the charitable sector.

Let us begin your journey on your path to nonprofit leadership.

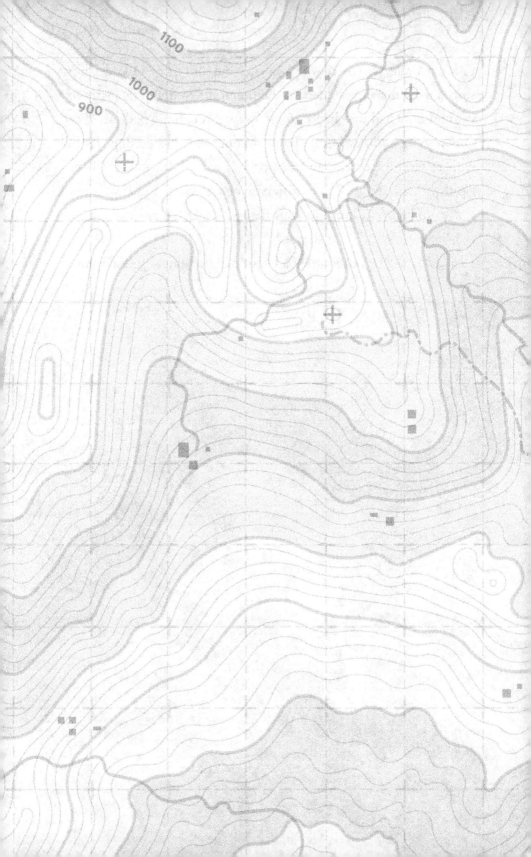

CHAPTER 2

Sharpen Your Vision

A s with any good strategic planning process, the first objective is to simply determine where you are going; as you ponder your journey along your path to nonprofit leadership, the objective here is no different. For many, however, this first step is often the hardest—and for good reason: you may not know exactly what nonprofit leadership looks like for you. That is okay. In this book, I will list and explain each step along the way. By the end, you will have a clear path to follow into the world of nonprofits.

This first stop along the path will equip you with the tools you need to *sharpen your vision*, even if you do not know exactly what your ultimate destination will be. As with each step along the path, I will detail the principles behind each one, share some real-life examples of individuals who have utilized the concept, and make sure you have practical tools to use and additional resources to consult as you build your personal strategic plan.

To best sharpen your vision, we will first describe the concepts of self-actualization and how they can both motivate and define your long-range plan. We will next discuss the three tools you will need to establish this crucial foundation of your plan, including an **annual personal retreat**, a commitment to various **journaling practices**, and, ultimately, the development of a **vision framework**, which is a foundational tool for the rest of your leadership journey.

Concepts

For many in the nonprofit sector, the challenge is not finding a cause about which they can be passionate but in understanding that the "grass is not always greener" once you get to the nonprofit side of the fence. Those aspiring to nonprofit leadership must thoughtfully consider the actual skills and experiences necessary for success in addition to the motivational elements of finding a good cause.

As you ponder your vision for nonprofit leadership, understanding your hierarchy of needs leads to an additional assessment of your intrinsic and extrinsic motivations:

- What drives you?

- Do you have the requisite knowledge, motivation, and organizational support to succeed in nonprofit leadership? Many aspiring candidates for the path bring endless motivational energy but may lack the knowledge and organizational support required, and thus many talented individuals are thwarted in their effort to achieve senior leadership.

Tool: Personal Planning Retreat

So how do you begin to sharpen your vision? The first step is to plan and conduct a personal planning retreat. You have likely participated in a variety of retreats and planning sessions with organizations that you are affiliated with, but most of the individuals I have worked with have not invested in a similar planning event for their personal strategic plan. Of course, we have all been part of painful planning retreats, too, and that is why the design and structure of this retreat should be carefully considered, so your journey on the path begins with a practical and motivational exercise that you will look forward to on an annual basis.

As much as any of the elements of your agenda while at the retreat, the greatest value will be in the concentrated time you spend on yourself and the intentional effort you devote to a distraction-free environment with enough time to recharge and ensure that you are physically and mentally engaged for the session.

What is the primary objective of your personal retreat? You want to establish a planning framework that will help you to map your course on the rest of the path and give yourself a working document that can be adopted and improved as you implement activity following the retreat.

The retreat provides a microcosm of your entire journey on the path:

- You will sharpen your vision and put your long-term goals and vision framework in writing.

- You will map your course and identify and assess the key skills and experiences you will need to achieve your ultimate leadership position.

- You will determine the key exercises you need to implement so that you can get in shape for the entire journey.

- You will create the curriculum you need to achieve short- and long-term learning by curating knowledge.

- You will begin to express yourself by practicing your personal case for support.

- You will build community by identifying the strategic partners you will need along your journey and the best way to engage them.

- And finally, you will identify any gaps in your résumé and find ways to practice leadership, even if your current position does not afford you many opportunities.

So how do you go about putting a personal retreat together? Consider these four steps:

1. **Start with the calendar.** How soon can you find two or three days that you could devote the time and energy to this effort? I find a weekend is often the best time to consider, which generally allows for a Friday afternoon travel period and a return home on Sunday evening. It can certainly occur at any time, but having a time buffer between your work and "real world" responsibilities is helpful, and having at least an overnight as part of the retreat assures a more refreshed approach as opposed to squeezing the session within your existing daily activities. Can this retreat be done in a one-day format? Yes, indeed, but I suggest that an abbreviated format is better for subsequent annual retreats or quarterly check-ins. The initial Personal Planning Retreat requires more time.

2. **Consider a location.** While it is not necessary to travel far, I strongly recommend a location outside of your usual home and work settings. You simply risk too many distractions and the pull of existing home and work chores if you remain local. If you are in the position to invest in a cabin, cottage, or bed-and-breakfast setting, then consider the money well spent. I find that a location within two to three hours from home is ideal, as the travel creates literal separation from my home base and also creates some time to decompress. However, if you are not in a position to invest in a location, consider your friend and family network. Who has a secondary residence or rental property that they might let you use?

3. **Invest some planning time in advance.** While the retreat will allow for spontaneous and creative thought, I maintain that there is great value in developing an agenda beforehand, gathering resource material in advance, and committing to some pre-retreat reading to set your mental framework. As far as an agenda (see Figure 1 for a sample agenda), I am less concerned about a minute-by-minute structure that adds pressure; rather, I focus on an overall framework that will motivate and help me to feel productive throughout the retreat. The retreat should basically be divided into six sections (begin vision framework, draft vision/mission statements and SWOT analysis, some outdoor activity/reflection, the Ten Essential Skills and Experiences worksheet, three strengths/weaknesses to build on, and then finalize vision framework), and you have the flexibility to shorten or extend each section, depending on your energy level. In the weeks leading up

to your retreat, I find it helpful to read a book or two that help set the stage for both the reflection you hope to do while away and also illustrate the long-term visioning you hope to accomplish.

In addition to the one or two books you will read beforehand, you may certainly bring other resource material to your retreat. For example:

- Your journal

- Your calendar

- Your current/last job description, annual plan/review

- Personal/family photographs or items that inspire

- Additional books you may reference or read

FIGURE 1: SAMPLE PERSONAL RETREAT AGENDA

Friday Evening: Vision Framework

Saturday Morning: Draft Vision/Mission Statements, SWOT Analysis

Saturday Afternoon: Outdoor Activity/Reflection

Saturday Evening: 10 Essential Nonprofit Leadership Skills & Experiences Assessment

Sunday Morning: 3 Strengths & Weaknesses to build on, three time horizons

Sunday Afternoon: Finish plan with 30/60/90 tactics; Finalize Vision Framework

4. **Manage the Logistics.** Since your goal is to achieve a highly productive retreat, you must ensure that the logistical elements are all in place and you are not tempted by the distraction of daily life. Pack weather-appropriate and comfortable clothing that allows for study and reflection as well as some outdoor and fitness activities. Plan your meals in advance, or at least ensure that you have access to restaurants and supplies for snacks and beverages as desired. The bottom line is that you do not want to waste time and mental energy chasing down basic supplies, so the more you can bring yourself or arrange in advance, the better.

If you cannot see a way to orchestrate such an outing in the next ninety days, then, by all means, adapt a one-day session at home or simply at a nearby location (library, coffee shop, etc.), where you can invest some quiet time and reflection around the core elements of the retreat, including the vision framework, the SWOT analysis, and the Ten Essential Nonprofit Leadership Skills and Experiences Assessment (more on that assessment in the next chapter). The personal retreat does not have to be an elaborate and expensive undertaking at an exotic location. However, given the importance of your long-term goals and desire to succeed on the path, I think an investment in a separate location is well worth it.

As a big fan of Cal Newport's *Deep Work*, I also think it is critical that you create or find an environment that is disturbance free. Of course, give family members a way to reach you, but if you are going to monitor email and social media throughout your retreat, then you might as well not do it.

Tool: Journaling

I am a big fan of journaling for reasons I will elaborate on later, but for the purpose of the retreat, the analog (and technology-free) nature of the journal is perfect.

If you have not been one to adopt a journaling practice, I highly recommend you give it a chance at your personal retreat. Once you begin to utilize it as a productivity tool, I think you will quickly see multiple applications that will only enhance your digital processes. As you contemplate a journaling practice (or are looking for ways to enhance your current practice), consider the following:

- Scientific research suggests that putting pen to paper is better for your cognitive recall. For example, scientists in Norway recently performed an experiment in which they compared participants who hand-wrote lists versus typing them; the results showed that participants had a significantly better free recall of words written in the handwriting condition compared to the keyboard condition.[3]

- Journaling is a great form of therapy and self-care. When I am wrestling with different situations or have ideas that are not fully formed, a free-form writing session often illuminates additional insight or helps to minimize the stress by getting it out of my head.

- In the spirit of curating knowledge and maintaining a lifelong learner status, I make it a point to write a brief summary of articles and books I have read and any presentations I attend.

---

3   Eva Ose Askvik, F. R. (Ruud) van der Weel, Audrey L. H. van der Meer, "The Importance of Cursive Handwriting over Typewriting for Learning in the Classroom: A High-Density EEG Study of 12-Year-Old Children and Young Adults," *Frontiers in Psychology* (July 2020), doi: 10.3389/fpsyg.2020.01810.

There is no doubt that I retain more of what I have heard or read if I force myself to explain it in my own words. For books, in particular, I have made it a habit to write a one-page summary for every book I have read in the last several years. My self-guided prompt is simply: "What are three takeaways from this book that might help me later?" This "book report" is usually no more than one page in my moleskin journal, and then I take a picture of the report and scan it into my Evernote program. Over the past few years, I have accumulated more than two hundred book reports that provide a wonderful library of content that I can incorporate into my writing, presentations, and recommendations to my coaching clients in response to their particular interests.

- Finally, your journal is a perfect place to sharpen your vision and put your personal strategic plan in place. Beginning with your personal vision and mission statement (which I explain in Tool: Vision Framework) and continuing with your goals and associated tactics, the journal is the perfect place to initiate the creative flow these things require. Once these items have been revised and edited on paper, I certainly like to convert them into a more permanent document by typing them up and printing them for my personal display. But the journal remains the best place to get my initial thoughts down without the temptation to self-edit that often occurs when using a keyboard.

> Your journal is a perfect place to sharpen your vision and put your personal strategic plan in place.

Tool: Vision Framework

While your personal retreat will allow you to expand on each element of the path (as outlined in the chapters that follow), the foundational tool you will be developing on your retreat is your vision framework. The vision framework allows you to articulate your goal of nonprofit leadership in a specific manner and provides a platform on which you build a sequence of activities to achieve your ultimate career position. What if your ultimate goal changes? No problem: your framework can adapt with you as your life circumstances evolve and new opportunities materialize. You will have confidence in knowing that your plan provides fundamental skills and experiences you need, even if specific elements change, such as your geographic parameters or the sector in which you might work.

Like any good strategic plan, the first element of your plan is a vision statement. While it should be relatively short in terms of word count, its motivational and directional importance cannot be understated. If you are reading this book, then it is likely that your professional vision is centered around a senior position—CEO, executive director, or president—of a nonprofit organization. Simply articulating that fact puts you ahead of most individuals (95 percent of the population does not have any *written* goals). Your clarity around senior leadership in the charitable sector is a good start. The power of the vision framework, however, is adding another layer of specificity to your vision statement so that the rest of your planning on the path has goals to target. "Senior leadership in the nonprofit sector" is a good place to start, but your vision will sharpen dramatically if you answer these six questions to expand your framework.

- What is your **timeline** for senior leadership on the path? This is obviously a relative concept, depending on where you currently stand in your nonprofit career. Generally, I suggest ten-, five-, or three-year timeframes to anchor your vision framework:

- If you are **new to the field** or a recent college graduate aspiring to nonprofit leadership: Start with a **ten-year framework** toward senior leadership.

- If you are a **midcareer professional** with five to ten years of experience: Start with a **five-year framework** toward senior leadership.

- If you are a **senior professional** on the verge of executive leadership: Start with a **three-year framework** to identify and land a CEO position.

- If you are a **lateral-entry candidate** (experienced professional from the for-profit sector with transferable skills): Start with a **three-year framework** to explore senior nonprofit leadership.

- In what nonprofit **sector** are you most comfortable? This could certainly change, but in an effort to move this plan from ideas in your head to an actionable document, consider which nonprofit sector you see the greatest potential in (e.g., arts and culture, human services, healthcare, education, faith-based, or environmental). If your focus is even more specific, use the added detail in your draft (e.g., K–12 education, career-related healthcare, a faith-based food ministry, etc.). Not sure? Just pick a sector that most resonates with you at this moment.

- What **geographic** parameters impact your vision? Your career path may well remain in the same community where you reside now, given family obligations or personal preference.

However, for the right opportunity, you might consider a relocation within your region, your state, or even your country. Depending on your flexibility on geography, make sure it is referenced in your vision framework, particularly if you have certain lifestyle and cultural elements you aspire to have (urban, suburban, rural).

- In what type of organizational **culture** do you want to work? This is an often overlooked element in creating a vision framework but is important to consider. The first question to consider is simply what size organization would be ideal for you—a large organization that offers diverse programs and more complex administration or perhaps a smaller organization that would allow your leadership to directly impact the staff, volunteers, and individuals you serve? Another cultural aspect is the affiliation of the organization. Is it an affiliate or chapter associated with a national or international organization, or is it an independent charity?

- What **educational** components will run parallel to your journey on the path? As a career-focused professional, you are likely focused on lifelong learning under any circumstance, but I believe this characteristic is significant enough to include in the vision framework. As the nonprofit sector evolves in its prominence and status for career opportunities, expectations for advanced degrees and sector-specific credentials will only increase. As such, I suggest that your educational vision be articulated with equal clarity. Is it likely that you will need a graduate degree to achieve your aspirational position? If not a requirement, it will certainly be preferred in almost all search processes. Certifications in fundraising, project management,

budgeting/finance, strategic planning, and board/volunteer management ought to be on your "educational wish list," regardless of current hiring requirements.

- What are your **financial** planning considerations for career placement? Compensation is likely not the driving force behind your pursuit of nonprofit leadership, but it is certainly reasonable to seek a salary that allows you to achieve financial stability by whatever metric makes sense to you. Do you have a spouse/partner who factors into a long-range financial plan? Children, parents, or other dependents? Again, this is just one element of your vision framework, but it is an important one to consider, as I have seen otherwise perfect career opportunities unravel because it did not provide the financial stability and potential for growth necessary for long-term success.

While there is much to consider in developing your vision framework, the thought and effort invested at this point on the path will pay off exponentially, as every part of your personal strategic plan will be anchored on distinct elements of your vision and ensure that you are moving in the right direction and obtaining the kind of résumé-building skills and experiences that your dream job will require.

So what does a vision framework look like? Let us consider an example based on each of the four leadership positions mentioned previously:

- Having just joined the nonprofit sector this year, my ten-year leadership vision for 2032 is to serve as executive director of a faith-based human services nonprofit anywhere in the state of North Carolina. I plan to obtain a master's degree, either an MBA or MPA, within the next five years. My preference is for an independent nonprofit with a smaller staff (fewer than twenty) that has compensation opportunities that are competitive but not necessarily at the top of the market.

> The thought and effort invested at this point on the path will pay off exponentially, as every part of your personal strategic plan will be anchored on distinct elements of your vision and ensure that you are moving in the right direction.

- With seven years of envisioning leadership opportunities, my five-year framework for 2027 is to become a CEO of a healthcare nonprofit, likely focused on seniors and our aging population. I recognize that this will likely be an affiliate or chapter of a national organization, and I am willing to relocate anywhere in the southeast United States. I enjoy traveling and would enjoy the diversity and complexity of a larger (fifty employees) organization. To round out my educational profile, I will enroll in a budget and planning certification at the local university and will seek a leadership position with our sector's professional association.

- As a senior administrator at three nonprofits over the past fourteen years, I am ready for a CEO opportunity as part of my vision framework by 2023. I want to remain in my community and continue to lead an arts and culture organization, preferably in the performance area. I will need to demonstrate more fundraising capability and will seek the CFRE certification next year. Having completed my MFA six years ago, I will seek a PhD through the hybrid program offered by my undergraduate alma mater.

- Having served as a volunteer and board chair for two nonprofits, I would like to explore a lateral move into a nonprofit CEO position in three years. Having achieved many of my financial goals, and with an early retirement opportunity, I am prepared to serve an organization that could use my skills to manage a newly merged entity and would accept a below-market salary to remain in the community. I plan to cochair a fundraising campaign for one of my current nonprofits, as well as lead a strategic planning effort for another to sharpen my skills. I will need an environment that has strong operational and programmatic staff leaders and one that can benefit from my management skills, community contacts, and willingness to fundraise.

While varied in their place on the path, their long-term objectives, and their current skills and experiences, each vision framework includes some degree of detail on each of the six components:

- Timeframe

- Sector

- Geography

- Culture

- Education

- Financial expectations

Armed with this level of detail, you have an incredibly valuable framework to build a comprehensive personal strategic plan, and every other stop on the path will have laser focus in its ability to support your plan, given its clarity.

Now that your vision is indeed sharpened, let us move ahead on the path and help you "map your course."

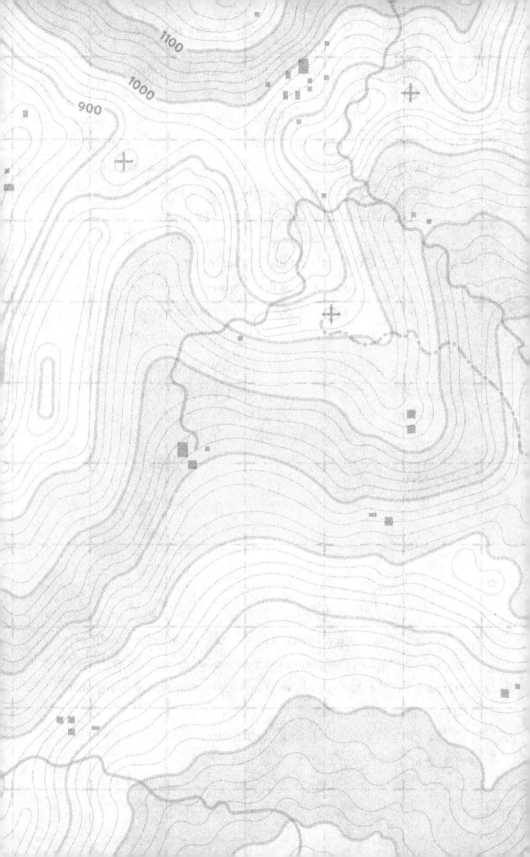

CHAPTER 3

Map Your Course

N ow that you have added clarity to your long-term career objectives through your vision framework and are motivated to put actionable steps into your plan, it is time to *map your course.* Your ultimate nonprofit leadership destination is clearer now that you have given thought to the six components that comprise the vision framework: timeframe, sector, geography, education, culture, and finances. These elements, individually and collectively, help you to define the specifics of your personal strategic plan. They will also help to ensure the most effective activities to achieve your goals and the most efficient, given the limits to your time and energy.

This chapter will help you to map your course by first helping evaluate where you are on the path and then providing an assessment tool so that you know exactly what strengths you will build on and what weaknesses you will need to overcome. Your assessment will also allow you to better understand the nonprofit environment in which you hope to work and then translate your assessment activities into a planning timeline that will factor in short-, medium-, and long-range objectives.

Concepts

Research on leadership success underscores the importance of self-awareness. It is critical that leaders have a high level of self-awareness because self-aware leaders can change their behavior to adjust to situations in which they find themselves. Self-aware leaders also recognize their own strengths, weaknesses, and blind spots and take accountability for them—this ability ultimately leads to higher levels of subordinate trust and satisfaction, which can ultimately lead to better organizational performance.

Tool: Ten Essential Nonprofit Leadership Skills and Experiences Assessment

Your first objective in mapping your course is to do a thorough self-assessment, measuring your current skills and experiences using the Ten Essential Nonprofit Leadership Skills and Experiences Assessment tool. To begin this exercise, reference the corresponding worksheet on my website at www.pattonmcdowell.com. This exercise will help increase your self-awareness about your leadership abilities. I have found the items listed on this chart to be vital for nonprofit professionals at any stage of their career, particularly for those aspiring to executive director and C-suite-level positions.

Note that mastery of these skills and experiences requires both the acquisition of relevant **content** for your leadership role (chapter 5,

"Curate Knowledge"), as well as practicing certain **skills** to demonstrate the requisite experience that hiring committees will be looking for and you must employ when managing your nonprofit organization.

Give yourself time to carefully evaluate each element in terms of your confidence in demonstrating the knowledge or skill required for senior leadership in each case. You will note the worksheet summarizes the definition of each skill or experience and allows space to write your self-evaluation statement as well as potential next steps or actions. Let us review each of the Ten Essential Skills and Experiences.

LEARNING PLAN

As discussed in chapter 2, within your vision framework, you should have an education track running parallel to your overall leadership path timeline. Having identified the likelihood of graduate education and/or other sector-specific and skill-enhancing certifications necessary for your nonprofit leadership goal, your assessment of a learning plan should detail these learning requirements and have them plotted over the next three, five, or ten years, depending on where you are on the path.

As with each of these ten skills and experiences, do not worry if you have not yet accomplished what is defined here or even if you are not sure exactly how success will be defined. Your process on the path will help you to expand your professional development activities if you are not sure or have not yet established your learning plan.

PERSONAL ORGANIZATION

I find that many nonprofit professionals approach task management as an endurance test and simply stay up later at night to get more done from their endless to-do list. However noble this might appear, working longer hours does not ensure true productivity, and as a nonprofit leader, it is infinitely more important that you are focused on the right things versus simply on more things.

I am a fan of David Allen's *Getting Things Done* (GTD) methodology,[4] but as you self-assess in this area of personal organization, it is less about a particular system and more about the fact that you have a system that allows you to accomplish your highest-priority objectives. For me, personal organization breaks down into three parts:

> As a nonprofit leader, it is infinitely more important that you are focused on the right things versus simply on more things.

- **Vision Framework**. My long-range goals are maintained in a visible format and reviewed daily. I use the OmniFocus app and automatically populate my daily to-do list with the same ten affirmations that remind me of my vision framework and key goals.

- **Weekly Review**. As espoused in the GTD framework, I am a proponent of the weekly review as a means to truly assess all of my to-do list items and make sure they are prioritized, delegated, or discarded. This process—every Saturday morning for me—ensures that the volume of the list does not dominate my view and that the most important items remain at the top.

- **Daily Targets**. Seldom does the to-do list ever get completed each day, but I make part of my morning routine to evaluate not only the to-do list for the day but also to identify the *three most important tasks* I must accomplish that day.

---

4   David Allen, *Getting Things Done: The Art of Stress-Free Productivity.* (New York: Penguin Books, 2015).

STRATEGIC PLANNING

While "strategic planning" is a phrase tossed around in nearly every organization, it is not necessarily a process that is fully understood or consistently applied within nonprofit settings. As a nonprofit leader, you will want to combine the diagnostic skill necessary to evaluate an organization's current state by bringing both a creative flair to help envision a successful future, and a discipline to build a plan that can actually make measurable progress.

The skill of strategic planning necessitates your understanding of the process, and three high-level components. As a thought exercise, you can apply these concepts to your current organization, even if you are not in a position to actually dictate the strategic plan, or you can apply these principles to another organization for which you volunteer or aspire to become more engaged.

The first question to answer as a strategic planner is simple: Can you articulate the organization's *vision* for success? Typically, this requires thought-provoking exercises and conversations with key stakeholders to creatively and ambitiously determine an aspirational plan that builds on the current mission and also assesses new growth potential and collaborative opportunities. How can an organization get better, *dramatically* better? How can your organization serve more of the people it wants to serve, or accomplish more of what it currently accomplishes—*much* more?

This kind of thinking is the visionary skill required for nonprofit leadership. I remember Mrs. Shriver's pride in the number of individuals Special Olympics International was serving, but also her intensity to reach those eligible individuals who were not yet benefitting from the program. Identifying the number of those not yet being served—and establishing a timeline to attract them into the program—became a compelling and actionable vision that was the platform for the strategic plan.

While providing an aspirational and inspirational vision is the first part of your strategic planning skillset, you must also be able to lead an effective *assessment* of an organization's current state. As you look at any nonprofit organization, what are the challenges that must be addressed first? What opportunities show the greatest promise for dramatic mission achievement? What threats must be contemplated, and which ones require contingency plans?

A classic SWOT (strengths, weaknesses, opportunities, and threats) analysis can help reveal many of the headlines for an assessment, and the same analysis can be applied to any element of an organization. You can easily practice performing a SWOT analysis by applying it to an area of your current job or volunteer responsibility. The real discipline required after an assessment is in the prioritization. It does an organization little good to just have a long list of items around each of the four SWOT components, because a much more meaningful assessment will also determine the most important items in each category. Consider adding an additional mental exercise to any planning activity of which you are a part by contemplating this question: What are the top three items in each SWOT category? Forced prioritization helps assure the most important items will be addressed first, and your ability to implement a plan will have greater clarity.

As a strategic planner, your next step after utilizing assessment criteria such as those mentioned above will be to assure effective *implementation*. Based on an assessment exercise and the resulting prioritization, what goals emerge? For each goal you contemplate, what is a reasonable timeline to achieve it? What specific tasks are required to achieve the goal? What resources are necessary to achieve the goal—specifically, who is responsible for overseeing the tasks that make up the goal's implementation? Make it your habit to ask these questions in any setting where a plan is involved, whether it be a process in which you are directly involved or one of which you are an observer.

Together, these strategic planning principles (*vision, assessment,* and *implementation*) comprise an essential skillset you must develop on your journey to nonprofit leadership.

NONPROFIT/SECTOR

It is easy to devote most, if not all, of your knowledge acquisition efforts to your current organization. However, your eventual leadership opportunities will be strengthened because those who will hire you trust that you can see beyond the "walls" of their singular organization. You must broaden your understanding to include others in your sector, as well as the issues that face the nonprofit sector in general.

First, within your sector, make sure that you become familiar with the local, state, and national associations with which your current or future nonprofit is associated. While each subsector varies, it is likely that your organization has some local affiliations through the United Way, an arts federation, or perhaps through a community foundation. See what organizations are involved, especially those that take leadership roles. Also, identify any associations in which your organization is a member on the state and national levels. These may include advocacy organizations that offer information, networking, and conferences.

> You must broaden your understanding to include others in your sector, as well as the issues that face the nonprofit sector in general.

An understanding of the landscape in which your organization is situated allows you to better understand the similarities and differences among your peer

45

organizations. Make it your goal to identify the differences among your peer institutions and contemplate how they adapt to the different variables every nonprofit must address: program scope, funding model, organizational size, and life stage and factors of geography and community influence. While a sector-wide analysis can be daunting, simply focus on identifying three organizations in two categories:

- What are the three organizations that would be considered "peer" organizations of yours—nonprofits that are closest to yours in size, scope, and mission?

- What are three organizations that would be considered "aspirational" organizations for yours—nonprofits that are considered "best in class" and ones that others in your sector would most like to emulate?

How do you determine these two categories of peer and aspirational organizations? In some sectors, state and national associations may lift up the top-performing organizations through organizational and individual awards and recognitions. However, an equally effective method is simply practicing your networking skills and asking senior leaders at your organization, as well as others whom you come in contact with: "What nonprofit do you think most closely resembles ours in our community/region/state?" This becomes a great conversation starter. Also consider an opening gambit such as this: "What nonprofit is considered the *best* in our community/region/state?" This will certainly prompt discussion and open doors for further give-and-take. Gathering this information improves your knowledge *and* your networking.

Your sector knowledge will expand dramatically if you maintain an awareness of your sector's peer and high-performing organizations. Beyond your sector, it is also important to be intentional about acquiring knowledge about nonprofit issues and topics in general. While you should be following your sector's primary periodicals, you should also look for information sources that explore the nonprofit sector in general, such as the *Chronicle of Philanthropy*, *Nonprofit Times*, *Stanford Social Innovation Review*, and *Nonprofit Quarterly*. It is also important to identify information sources at your state and local levels. A good place to start is your closest community foundation as well as your state's Center for Nonprofits.

FINANCIAL ACUMEN

Most nonprofit professionals enter the field with—or quickly acquire—a passion for the mission and program their organization delivers. Often, this passion translates well to marketing and fund development opportunities that rely on an ability to articulate the fundamental purpose of the organization to various stakeholder groups. These relational skills are considered important to your eventual senior leadership on the path, but they are not actually required for success to the same degree as is financial mastery. This is not to suggest that you need an accounting/finance degree to successfully serve as an executive director, but you must be competent at budget management and the associated profit-and-loss statements, balance sheets, and overarching financial evaluations, such as your nonprofit's audit and its IRS Form 990.

For those of you coming from a liberal arts degree like I did, do not panic. Most nonprofit organizations have access to accounting and finance talent, either on staff or through an accounting firm. The fact remains, however, that you must have enough financial acumen to comfortably discuss these issues with the appropriate staff, board, and accounting professionals who will be associated with your nonprofit.

Approach this knowledge area in two ways: academic and practical. On the academic side, design a curriculum for yourself in this area; commit to learning the basics of accounting through text or online resources. Understand three basics of financial management and be able to define and distinguish between the P + L, the balance sheet, and the statement of cash flow. In addition to your personal curriculum of resources, take a basic finance course online or through a local university or community college. I ultimately determined that the pursuit of a graduate degree (MBA) would force me to learn these finance and accounting basics, and it gave me the confidence to "talk the talk" at the senior level.

The second part of your financial education should be practical: use your *own* organization as the primary teaching tool. Many nonprofit professionals, especially early in their careers, may not be required to understand their organization's budget or financial details. Even if that is the case, force yourself to learn the key drivers of your organization's financial health. Here are three ways you can do that:

- Talk to your organization's chief financial officer. The CFO will be grateful that you are asking about something other than wrestling for more budget resources. Ask the following questions: "What are the three key revenue drivers to our organizational health, and where can I track them on the budget?" Similarly, ask about the three key expense drivers that impact the bottom line and where exactly they show up on the organization's financial statements. By understanding those six factors, you will be more informed than most of your staff colleagues, and you will also gain valuable experience talking to a CFO and better understand where they are coming from (which is a critical relationship you will have to manage when you are a CEO).

- Ask to attend the finance committee meeting of the board as an observer, if possible. Perhaps your "new best friend," the CFO, will appreciate your efforts to better understand the organization's finances and will not only let you observe but also give you a preview of the material and reports that are prepared for the board so that you can better understand the meeting objectives and anticipate the nature of the discussion. Again, if you are sincere in your efforts and respectful of their time, the CFO may also provide a review of the meeting and highlight some of the questions and discussion that occurred, and help you to understand the nuances of the session that may not have been clear to you during the meeting. By designing a "self-orientation" such as this to your organization's finances, you will not only become a more engaged observer of all future staff and board meetings that involve the budget, but you will also begin to craft your own approach to budget management and financial reporting that you will ultimately control as CEO.

- Your final exercise toward this crash course in financial acumen is to review copies of your nonprofit's IRS Form 990 and most recent audit, both of which should be publicly available. Your CFO colleague may prove to be the best guide for understanding both documents unless you are able to review them with the CEO. For most organizations, both of these documents are often relegated to a check box on the board's agenda, and limited discussion follows. However, in your eventual senior leadership role, you must truly understand what is involved in both documents, as their public nature subjects you and your nonprofit to potential scrutiny.

The fact remains that most of your nonprofit colleagues—who are not within the finance or business office of the organization—are not going to volunteer to engage with the organization's budget, the board's finances, or the nonprofit's fiduciary reports. However, as you pursue success on your path to nonprofit leadership, your orientation into finance and accounting will be a differentiator when your CEO candidacy is considered.

SPEAKING

Public speaking typically ranks low on individuals' lists of things they *like* to do. However, it is a skill that nonprofit leadership will require as a means to communicate with internal staff and board audiences as well as external audiences, including special events and media opportunities. Depending on your current role, the chance to practice extemporaneous public speaking or prepared presentations may vary, but gaining additional practice should be part of your plan going forward. Honestly assess your current comfort level speaking before a full staff or board meeting or an even larger audience at your nonprofit's annual gala or at a national conference of fellow professionals.

While public speaking need not be your favorite activity, it is a skill that you can and should develop over time, first in smaller group settings and then in larger groups as you elevate your public speaking proficiency. I recommend that you focus on three elements:

- **Audience analysis**. Who exactly is in your audience, and what do they need to take away from your remarks? Your audience is likely looking for concise comments with clear action steps or key questions that must be answered. Before speaking, consider framing your comments just as you would an effective memo: headline, supporting points, conclusion. I am always impressed with colleagues who understand their internal audience (including their boss) and deliver their comments in meeting settings in an organized manner. In large or small settings: What does your audience hope to take away from your remarks?

- **Presentation structure**. While impromptu settings such as staff or board meetings do not allow for extended preparation, the "memo design" remains a great approach (headline, supporting points, summary) to collect your thoughts before raising your hand. When given time to prepare, your framework as a presenter is not dissimilar to your impromptu speaking structure:

  □ Headline: What are you speaking about, and what story will "hook" your audience?

  □ What are the three points/examples you can give to reinforce your headline?

  □ Summary: What call to action can you best illustrate to make your point and inspire your audience?

- **Delivery**. Understanding your audience and a well-designed structure will help your confidence when delivering an effective public presentation. Find opportunities to practice your delivery in large-group settings by introducing a speaker at your large events or perhaps volunteering to introduce a session at a conference. Once you have some experience, you can begin to evaluate the fundamentals of your public speaking delivery:

  □ Pace—Are you speaking too fast?

  □ Volume—Are you speaking clearly so everyone can hear?

       □ Engagement—Are you making eye contact with the audience?

WRITING

Successful nonprofit leadership will require you to communicate in a variety of written formats. Like public speaking, your enthusiasm for writing may be mixed, but it is a skill that you must develop for maximum impact. Consider the following four types of writing with which you should be comfortable:

- **Narrative**. Put your story and your organization's story in writing. Your ability to effectively describe a narrative event or background will enhance all forms of communication.

- **Persuasive**. As the leader of your nonprofit, your voice will be critical in all of your organization's calls to action, and most will first be delivered in writing. Whether it be an effort to recruit a staff/board member to join your organization or crafting an effective case for support for a grant application, a critical element will likely be written.

- **Business memo**. In contrast to a narrative or persuasive writings, a business memo is a format necessary to convey information about your organization in a concise, factual, and easy-to-digest fashion. Many of your board members will not invest time in extended reading assignments and will require you to summarize the salient points in this type of brief, focused writing.

- **Personal note**. Do not underestimate the power of a hand-written note and your ability to deliver an authentic and personalized form of written communication. Handwriting is essential, but do not worry about how good it is. Simply make sure the note is legible and spelled correctly. That's what counts. A handwritten note shows that you took the time to send your thanks properly. Handwriting elevates a thank-you letter, whether to a donor, to a mentor, or after an interview. It is a classy gesture that will be appreciated by the recipient.

LISTENING/CONVERSATION

While much of our focus in the area of communication is justifiably centered around the delivery of written and spoken content, we often overlook the ability to be an effective *listener*. Listen two-thirds of the time while only speaking one-third. This advice is true in many professional settings, particularly when you are networking and trying to make a good impression. Listening is paramount. Focus completely on the interaction:

- Are you making eye contact, or are you staring over the speaker's shoulder?

- Are you being an active listener through verbal affirmation or body language?

- Do you repeat key information for clarity and confirmation?

- Do you pose thoughtful follow-up questions that allow your colleague to expand on their thoughts?

- Do you interrupt before they finish what they are saying?

The point, of course, is that a favorable impression you seek is often delivered because of your active listening skills as much as—if not more so than—how you communicate. Ask a friend or a colleague to give you an honest appraisal of your listening skills. Often, negative habits—like interrupting someone who is speaking or obviously waiting for them to finish so you can talk—are inadvertent and can be consciously improved once noted.

NETWORKING

Nonprofit leadership requires an ability to identify and engage with key individuals in varied networks who are associated with your organization. While it is easy to keep your head down and focus on the tasks directly related to your nonprofit, your organization needs you to stay abreast of issues that face your sector, your community, and the different constituencies you serve. In the broadest sense, "networking" can imply an endless stream of activities that involve mindless small talk at after-work functions, which are not the best use of your time. Effective, *strategic* networking, however (explored more thoroughly in chapter 7, "Build Community"), is best accomplished in a thoughtful and efficient manner:

- What other nonprofit leaders serve the same population your organization does? Can you identify three such leaders whom you admire who could offer timely insight?

- Who are the most respected donors and volunteers who support your cause?

- Who are some of the key community leaders who influence policy and the public discourse around your organization's mission?

As you self-evaluate your networking skills, start with identifying those individuals in each of these categories. I suggest your primary list of networking targets not exceed ten people, and an effective communication network can be maintained by connecting with one or two of them each month.

LEADERSHIP

While your primary goal is to achieve nonprofit leadership, you must find opportunities to practice leadership on all levels to make the case that you are qualified to lead at the top. If your challenge is that your current position does not afford you traditional leadership responsibility in terms of other staff members reporting to you, there are still multiple ways you can practice leadership to illustrate that experience to a future employer. We will review these opportunities in more detail in chapter 8, "Practice Leadership," but as you complete this self-assessment, consider the following:

> While it is easy to keep your head down and focus on the tasks directly related to your nonprofit, your organization needs you to stay abreast of issues that face your sector, your community, and the different constituencies you serve.

- What projects have you managed (or could manage) that demonstrate your ability to deliver results within time and budget constraints?

- Are you helping manage any events that require the collaborative leadership of other staff colleagues and volunteer leaders?

- Are you serving on any staff or board committees that could allow you to take a leadership role and allow you to volunteer your efforts to lead a particular initiative?

- Equally important to your potential leadership opportunities within your current organization are the organizations you are involved with outside of work. Volunteer-driven organizations are *always* in need of leadership if you are willing to raise your hand. If you are already investing your time attending meetings and supporting various activities, then you might as well lead the meetings yourself.

Now that you have been oriented to the ten skills and experiences necessary for successful nonprofit leadership, take the time necessary (perhaps on your personal planning retreat) to honestly evaluate each of these elements by using the associated worksheet. In chapter 4, "Get in Shape," you organize and prioritize a plan to build on those areas where you excel and address those areas that need work.

Get in Shape

N ow that you have mapped your course and begun to honestly appraise the skills and experiences you need to succeed, it is time to activate your plan. "Activation" continues to build on the strategic vision you have established and now has a more tangible set of skills and experiences that can either be maximized as existing strengths or addressed if they emerge as weaknesses.

This chapter will help you get in shape by first evaluating your strengths and weaknesses—based on the Ten Essential Skills and Experiences assessment from chapter 3—and identifying specific tactics for how to improve them. Second, you will learn about the importance of maximizing your time and energy, where I include rituals and systems as tools for boosting productivity.

Concept: Identifying Your Strengths and Weaknesses

Many annual reviews and evaluations in work settings tend to focus on weaknesses, but in this strategic planning process on the path, we intentionally start by identifying your strengths, which can often be leveraged for greater potential, rather than only focusing on areas of weakness. Why do we take this "strengths-forward" approach? Research shows that strengths-based leader mindsets can lead to both increased motivation and performance. A study done by Gallup[5] found that by focusing on developing strengths, participants reported higher levels of confidence, productivity, and self-awareness. Furthermore, Carol Dweck—Stanford professor and researcher who has popularized the concept of the "growth mindset"—argues that believing that your talents (i.e., strengths) can be developed is just as important as believing that your weaknesses can be improved.[6] So in this activation process, we identify *both* our strengths and weaknesses and how to improve.

If you are a comfortable public speaker, for example, and consider it one of your strengths, then your immediate question must be: "How can I utilize this skill to enhance my professional standing?" Continuing with that example, here are four ways you might leverage that strength:

- Identify existing staff and board meetings where you could be given an opportunity to provide an update or be part of a presentation.

---

5   "Strengths Development & Coaching," Gallup, www.gallup.com/learning/248405/
    strengths-development-coaching.aspx.

6   Jessica Greene, "Work on Your Strengths, Not Your Weaknesses," Zapier, May 9,
    2019, https://zapier.com/blog/how-to-find-your-strengths/.

- Inquire whether your organization has a special event during which you could offer even a small part of the agenda by introducing a speaker or making an announcement.

- Identify other organizations—community, faith-based, volunteer—that might offer you a chance to speak, present, or emcee.

- Discern opportunities to speak at conferences or professional meetings you are attending.

TOOL: PERSONAL SWOT ANALYSIS

After you have completed the Ten Skills Worksheet, the first step to defining your plan is to filter the skills and experiences on the worksheet through the personal SWOT (strengths, weaknesses, opportunities, and threats) analysis worksheet (also found on my website, www.pattonmcdowell.com). As you consider all ten elements of the skills/experiences worksheet, which two would you consider your strongest? Which two would you consider your weakest? Place these four items in their respective boxes on the personal SWOT worksheet. While all ten elements remain important for your overall leadership profile—and will be reviewed on a regular basis—it is unrealistic to address all ten simultaneously.

The point is your personal SWOT worksheet should not only help you lift up your two professional strengths but also identify two specific activities that help you build on them and achieve your skill or experience goal. A three-part process emerges:

- Goal: Maximize your SWOT strength of public speaking.

- Strategy: Identify two or three opportunities in the next year to be "on stage."

- Tactic: In the next ninety days, contact organizers for each of your target speaking opportunities, and inquire how you might help.

Similarly, the SWOT worksheet should also allow you to prioritize the two professional weaknesses you must first address. Using a similar goal-setting design as you utilized in framing your strength-based activities, your weaknesses can be addressed in a similar fashion:

- Goal: Strategically address your SWOT weakness of limited financial acumen.

- Strategy: Identify two or three content sources and experts who can help you confidentially explain your organization's finances.

- Tactic: Seek meetings with the CFO and board treasurer for a high-level orientation after a prior review of the organization's budget and Form 990.

The personal SWOT analysis will help you to determine what "muscles" you most need to exercise, building on your strengths and identifying targeted exercises for those muscles least in use. The SWOT exercise also provides two other strategic lenses through which to look at your career plan and assessment: the **opportunities** and **threats** quadrants. While the first two quadrants focused on skills and experiences you can address yourself, the next two areas cannot be managed directly but still have a significant impact on your career journey.

The opportunities quadrant requires you to carefully consider what options might emerge for you professionally on multiple levels:

- Within your organization, do you anticipate changes vertically (your boss) or horizontally (other departments) that might offer opportunities for you?

- Within your sector, what peer organizations might offer opportunities based on changes in leadership or structural changes, such as a merger?

- Depending on your vision framework's geography parameters, what peer organizations across the state, region, or country might be worthy of your consideration if the right opportunity emerges?

While less pleasant to consider, the personal SWOT also allows you to contemplate "threat" scenarios beyond your control. What would you do if you had to face a new boss or board chair who was not viable for you? What if you were the casualty of an organizational downsizing or a budget cut or were simply let go? Ideally, a job change will come as a result of an attractive opportunity, but it is prudent to at least consider difficult scenarios, so you are not completely blindsided.

Concept: Maximizing Your Productivity

The next step for getting in shape is to thoroughly evaluate your overall productivity in every personal and professional setting. It is worth noting the use of the term *productivity*, in this case, is highly subjective and does not suggest you become a robotic machine that gets up early and stays up late seven days a week, churning activity. In fact, productivity is more about identifying the *right* things to do and having the mental and physical energy to do them in a space and time full of clutter and distraction.

This productivity definition seems pretty straightforward, but it has multiple elements that you can evaluate and improve if necessary:

- Personal organization system

- Rituals and systems

- Whole-person scorecard: Diet, sleep, exercise focus

A personal organization system first requires an assessment of where all of the incoming data, information, and material comes from in your life and how you organize—and prioritize—it. Again, you must ensure that you are doing the most important things for your personal and professional success and not getting lost in the volume of inputs. As discussed in the Ten Skills and Experiences Worksheet, the ability to excel in the personal organizational process is a critical component that separates the most successful nonprofit leaders from all the rest.

> Productivity is more about identifying the *right* things to do and having the mental and physical energy to do them in a space and time full of clutter and distraction.

As mentioned, I am a proponent of David Allen's GTD approach, which has as a fundamental tenet that your task list should *not* be divided into subcategories such as "work" and "home." This is certainly a personal preference, but your overall productivity and peace of mind are contingent upon your accomplishing *all* of your important tasks, at work or at home. There is more risk of something falling through the cracks with multiple to-do lists and more associated psychic stress.

The next things to consider are the various inputs that create tasks for you to do. Primarily, these fall into two broad categories:

1. Digital inputs: emails, texts, phone messages

2. Physical inputs: mail, printed material, files

While this book does not address each of the inputs at a granular level, the goal is to evaluate each of them and ensure the accuracy and efficiency of each input moving into your task list when an action is required. While not always practical, perhaps your goal should be to address each input within twenty-four hours in the best-case scenario and not later than one week in a worst-case scenario. A quick self-test is simply to ask this question: Do you have emails, texts, phone messages, physical mail, or documents that are older than one week without any type of action? If so, that is an element of your system that must be addressed in your next ninety-day plan.

As most productivity gurus suggest, this does not mean you must robotically address every input the moment it comes in, which of course dramatically diminishes your productivity as you become distracted by every email, text, and alert that hits your device constantly. As we will discuss next in rituals and systems, this means that you are proactive about when and how you will address each input and that you have a system to either *do it, discard it, delegate it,* or *defer it.* Be intentional about each process, and honestly evaluate where the delays occur. By breaking down each of your inputs, you can be thoughtful about how you capture them, prioritize them, and get them done.

TOOL: PHYSICAL DECLUTTERING RITUAL

I have found it particularly helpful to commit to a monthly "declutter" routine. Typically, this is an hour during the weekend when I review the physical piles of material that have accumulated on my work and home desks. The longer I allow the stuff to gather, the more difficult and time consuming it is to organize, which is especially frustrating when I urgently require an item. If you have not decluttered your life in a while, you might consider a two- or three-hour session to start, and scale it back to an hour a month once you ritualize the process. It is certainly not the most entertaining activity on the weekend, but there is a cathartic benefit to the process. Turn on some music, grab a trash can and a recycling bin, put *everything* into one pile, and get started. Resist the urge to actually *do* anything that the material requires. For now, to get to the bottom of the pile, simply commit to sorting material into one of four categories:

- Trash/Recycle
- File/Scan
- Read/Review
- Action Required

After enduring the first foray in decluttering, you will ideally maintain a monthly or weekly routine that will help you to stay on top of the potential clutter in your life and be more productive as a result.

TOOL: DIGITAL DECLUTTERING RITUAL

Of course, much of the inputs and content you must manage are not physical items but are electronic; address these with a similar mindset to declutter, and then determine those items requiring action. The immediacy that many of these digital inputs create can make it difficult to stay focused on your most productive tasks, but this is where an organized structure of rituals and systems can really pay off.

Put on your calendar one hour each week to carefully review the previous week's activity. I do this every Saturday morning, asking a built-in question: "Is there any follow-up task for which I am responsible?" Perhaps I owe a thank-you note, an email follow-up, or a forwarded email to a colleague. There is inevitably something I need to capture as an input that requires action. Similarly, I review emails, voice messages, and social media alerts from the previous week to gauge whether any further responses are required or whether something can now be done, delegated, or deleted. In roughly thirty minutes, I am able to declutter virtually all of my electronic inputs, and then I turn my attention to the week ahead.

TOOL: PROACTIVE CALENDAR MANAGEMENT AND TIME-BLOCKING

Once I have decluttered, I can complete a visual review of each day's calendar in the week ahead and the various meetings, calls, and events, with a conscious effort to prioritize items I am responsible for and identify who else might require information in advance, and who might be a resource by delegating a related task. Some of the busiest yet most productive nonprofit leaders with whom I have worked are especially adept at *managing* their calendars instead of *reacting* to them. Certainly, there are some incidences where you simply must make time for your boss, your board chair, or a key donor who calls on you. But a proactive calendaring approach seeks meetings in advance with key leaders in your organization and also blocks time around their typically preferred meeting times. Your board chair or boss may well be a moving target in terms of scheduling a meeting, but sometimes suggesting a meeting time that is likely available on their schedule is a good approach versus waiting for the last-minute request. See if you can proactively get critical meetings set in ninety-day increments so that you can have some calendar certainty and then build around these VIP sessions.

Many of the leaders I have interviewed on the podcast are quick to point out the value of time-blocking, especially when it comes to ensuring that time is allowed for actually completing tasks. It is easy to fall victim to a calendar that is filled with meeting after meeting but without sufficient time built in your calendar to prepare for and respond to the meetings themselves. Some of the best approaches to time-blocking include:

- No meetings at all on a certain day or during a certain part of the day. This can be even more effective if an entire organization adopts a "no-meeting Wednesday" or restricts any internal meetings before 10:00 a.m. if early mornings are collectively determined as the most productive for individuals. A corollary of the no-meeting rule is to seek organization-wide agreement on having *all* standard meetings on the same day each week, thus freeing up other days from interruption. Maybe your organization might declare Tuesdays as the only day to schedule the weekly staff meeting or standard one-on-one meetings with direct reports.

- Perhaps the most vital time-blocking tactic is preventing any outside distractions or meeting requests during your most productive times. Literally block in your calendar as "busy" during the times that allow you the most productive reading, research, writing, or presentation prep. While emergencies do occur, the best leaders protect this productivity time with the same intensity they would any other important meetings. If you are relying on after-hour periods and weekends to get your highest-quality work done, then you are likely diminishing your effectiveness by wearing yourself out, as well as limiting your margins for family and personal balance.

- A final point about time-blocking is finding time away from the daily grind of your work. Can you devote one day a month to getting out of your office mindset to literally spend time thinking? A day of quiet reflection on your personal and professional strategic plan can in many ways be the most productive day you will spend each month, but this type of calendar investment is often put off—month after month—because

there is too much day-to-day work to do. The fact is that you will *never* finish enough of your strategic availability. Whether you literally leave town to assure separation from your work environment or simply stay off of your devices to avoid temptation, make sure you proactively calendar time for generative thinking and to simply recharge your batteries.

TOOL: WHOLE-PERSON SCORECARD

Speaking of your "batteries" and the energy necessary to be an effective nonprofit leader, your plan should prominently feature health and wellness. While there are technically no physical fitness requirements in most senior nonprofit job descriptions, I am convinced that the most successful leaders understand the long-term productivity benefits of their mental, physical, and emotional energy levels. But equally important is the effect these have on your satisfaction and self-actualization as a leader and a person. While there is a multitude of resources to address your "whole-person scorecard," for the purposes of the path to nonprofit leadership and in my coaching of nonprofit leaders, I ask the following questions:

- *Are you getting enough quality sleep?* The fact is that most of us are not, and some may view our ability to survive with less sleep as a badge of toughness. Science is still uncovering the hidden benefits of quality sleep, and if your routine does

> I am convinced that the most successful leaders understand the long-term productivity benefits of their mental, physical, and emotional energy levels.

not currently provide it, then you must factor sleep into your plan.

- Similarly, *do you have an exercise routine?* This is not only a vital part of your long-term health, but is also directly correlated to your short-term creativity, productivity, and the energy that can be devoted to working. Especially with the increase of remote (and sedentary) work, you must be even more intentional about getting your body in motion on a regular basis. Whether you favor high-intensity interval training or simply walking around the block, consider your current state of fitness and add some activity to your calendar, just as you would any other vital meeting or endeavor.

- Sleep and exercise certainly influence your productivity and energy levels, but do not forget diet. Again, too much information is available for me to summarize here, but the question is still valid as you ponder your leadership journey: *Are you eating healthily?* What can you do to improve your daily rituals to ensure that you eat better and improve your short- and long-term health as a result?

- Finally, your whole-person scorecard includes an exploration of your mindfulness practices. Just as the science about the restorative value of sleep is still emerging, so similar benefits are becoming apparent around the value of mindfulness and meditation. *Do you give yourself the benefit of quiet time?* We seldom find time without our minds racing, and our daily routine is simply an alarm-clock start followed by a sprint to a nightly collapse. Many good resources exist, and you owe it to yourself to explore some form of deep breathing, meditation, and variations that include yoga and walking.

Getting in shape as a nonprofit leader takes a significant commitment of time and the discipline to stay the course for the long haul when so many pressures and distractions push you into a short-term, reactive mode. Consider each of the components in this chapter: your systems of productivity and input management; your ability to declutter the volume of content you organize; and your consideration of a personal scorecard to include sleep, exercise, diet, and mindfulness practices. Not one of these components is something you can simply check off your list and forget, but *each* is a critical ongoing element that ties *directly* to your success in nonprofit leadership.

In the next chapter on the path, we will explore the concept of "curating knowledge" and how you will build a curriculum of content to help you move forward.

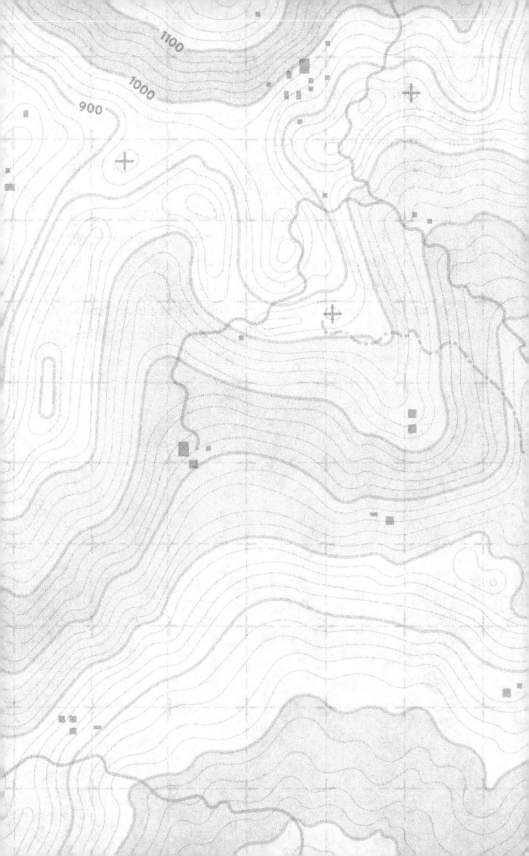

CHAPTER 5

Curate Knowledge

Your journey along the path will continue to accelerate as you get clarity around your vision, reflect on your key strengths and challenges, and build the stamina to successfully move forward. Just as each step along the path requires ongoing attention, this chapter highlights an area of particular importance to nonprofit leaders—the ability to identify and comprehend *current* information that is vital to your professional process. Of course, two challenges emerge as you endeavor to stay informed in an age of overwhelming amounts of information bombarding you every day. The first challenge is identifying the *right* information to collect, and the second challenge is having the time and mental energy to absorb what you must know. This chapter helps you to build on the principles of the earlier chapters to establish a system to curate knowledge that will keep you on the cutting edge of your profession.

There are five concepts to explore as you build a system for curating knowledge:

- Job mapping

- Networking insights

- Foundational library

- Relevant resources

- Deep work practices

Job Mapping

As you find more clarity around the type of leadership role you aspire to fulfill, your sharpened focus should allow you to identify specific positions (and their job descriptions) so you can learn more. I suggest you create an electronic file folder where you begin to collect any job description or summary you can find of leaders you admire or positions in which you might have interest in some day.

This exercise is the first step toward curating the overall knowledge you need to achieve senior leadership and maintain success once you get there. Your job description "collection" allows you to study the primary and secondary requirements your ideal job will require:

- What are the primary responsibilities listed for this position?

- What level of experience is required, and for how long must you have served in that type of role?

- What specific education, certification, or credential is required or preferred?

- What technical skills and experiences are required or preferred?

- What other organizational characteristics or cultural aspects can you ascertain based on the description?

By reviewing these aspirational job descriptions with a candidate's mindset (even if you are years away from actually applying), you turn this "collection" into a proactive and practical exercise for curating knowledge. Using these five questions as a review process, you will begin to see more clearly the critical skills, experiences, and knowledge required to compete for these types of senior leadership positions. Your skills assessment work from chapter 3 should have already oriented you to some of the areas on which you should focus. This job-mapping routine will further sharpen your focus on the knowledge you must attain to succeed in your particular sector.

Networking Insights

While much of your efforts to curate knowledge will come through classic reading and studying techniques, some of the most important knowledge will come from strategic networking, discussed in more detail in chapter 8, "Practice Leadership." Simply put, every conversation with leaders in your sector is an opportunity to gain knowledge directly and indirectly. Do not miss these opportunities to understand the information and motivation behind their journey to success.

With direct information, I am always looking to understand the component parts that came together to help other leaders to achieve success. What *skills* do they consider most important to their current leadership, what *knowledge* do they most have to call upon in their current role, and what *experiences* best prepared them for the work they do now?

> You will begin to see more clearly the critical skills, experiences, and knowledge required to compete for these types of senior leadership positions.

It is an easy conversation starter to ask leaders if they have read any good books lately, but it may be more instructive to ask, "What have been some of the most helpful books to you in terms of career development?" or, "What do you recommend I read to help me with [specify a skill or knowledge area about which you want to get better]?" Of course, these questions may not necessarily lead to books but rather to individuals, courses, workshops, or other resource material. That is an equally positive outcome and further builds your knowledge base.

Finally, utilize each networking contact to determine how they stay current on relevant topics in their sector, community, or other leadership arena. Find out what newsletters or electronic bulletins they pay close attention to. What blogs, websites, or podcasts they follow. Who they consider a thought leader in their world. These types of conversations do not happen every day, but when you do have the chance to have a deeper discussion with someone ahead of you on the path, there is no reason you do not come away with multiple resources to add to your "library" and further curate knowledge.

Foundational Knowledge

Your self-assessment, job mapping, and networking insights should all contribute to an understanding of the fundamental concepts that you must understand to succeed as a nonprofit leader. For every skill and experience represented on the Ten Skills Worksheet, there are multiple foundational texts suggested in the "Relevant Resources" section following this one, at least one of which should be read and maintained in your library.

This is, of course, a subjective list of what I believe are fundamental texts, and you may well supplement or replace certain selections based on your own research and acquired recommendations. Simply put, you want to ensure that you are grounded in the fundamentals of every leadership trait or characteristic and have a reliable resource to turn to if a question were to emerge. Your library can and will expand as you balance between the latest publications and new ways of thinking about these topics and the "classics" that define the fundamentals.

Relevant Resources

While you remain grounded by the foundational texts that provide a platform for your leadership journey, you must also create a system to ensure that you are attuned to the latest thought leadership and scholarship on topics related to your role. While all ten of the key skills and experiences can produce new material and new ways of thinking, five of them ought to be of particular interest as you add to your fundamental library with a section that welcomes the latest releases.

- **Leadership**. While you should be grounded in the teachings of Peter Drucker and Ram Charan, you should also be on the lookout for new perspectives on leadership and management from practitioners and scholars through periodicals such as the following:

    □ *Harvard Business Review, HBR IdeaCast*

    □ *Stanford Social Innovation Review*

    □ *Lead to Win* podcast

- **Personal organization**. As the volume of information increases and technology platforms multiply, it pays to stay on top of the latest tips and tricks that may help you continue to improve your personal organizational skills. Several resources I have found helpful:

- *Beyond the To-Do List* podcast, by Erik Fisher

- *The Productivity Show*, by Asian Efficiency

- *Getting Things Done* podcast

- *Deep Questions with Cal Newport*

- **Nonprofit sector**. Obviously, as a nonprofit leader, you need to stay apprised of issues facing the sector as a whole but also headlines specific to the subsector in which you work (i.e., education, arts and culture, healthcare) as well as issues that affect your community and region. In terms of nonprofit resources in general, email subscriptions to several of these e-newsletters make sense:

  - *The Chronicle of Philanthropy*

  - *BoardSource SmartBrief*

  - AFP Weekly and Daily Updates

  - *Blue Avocado* Monthly Issues

  - Sector-specific publications from associations

  - Local/regional publications from community foundations, local AFP chapters, United Way, and Arts Federations

  - Giving USA

- **Strategic planning and management**. In addition to the leadership principles that are shared through outlets, there is also value in the lessons learned from others, particularly creative managers and innovators who are addressing real-world challenges, regardless of profession. I find great value in biographical insights from websites and audio outlets that curate this type of information.

- *Do Your Good*, with Sybil Ackerman-Munson
- *Successful Nonprofits Podcast*, with Dolph Goldenburg
- *Nonprofit Jenni Show*, with Jenni Hargrove
- *Nonprofit Leadership Podcast*, with Rob Harter
- *Inspired Nonprofit Leadership*, with Mary Hiland
- *The Fundraising Talent Podcast*, with Jason Lewis
- *Let's Take This Offline*, with Kishshana Palmer
- My podcast, *Your Path to Nonprofit Leadership*

Deep Work Practices

While each of these prior steps will help you to identify the right kinds of content to succeed on your leadership journey, the true value of curating knowledge is ensuring that you can absorb the most relevant information and utilize it when necessary. To achieve this practical application of your curated knowledge, you must initiate routines that allow you time to review the constant stream of information; even though you have created a more streamlined system of relevant source material, you still must discern which information warrants additional

> The true value of curating knowledge is ensuring that you can absorb the most relevant information and utilize it when necessary.

study. Here are three rituals that can help transfer volumes of data into a useful application:

- **Daily scan and capture**. Most of your relevant resources come to you electronically as email alerts. Based on the headlines or summary description, the immediate evaluation is whether the information appears to fall into a category of interest to you. At a minimum, you can simply create an inbox folder within your email provider and store the item there. To be more proactive, you could create broad categories for different inbox folders to correspond with your library categories, such as leadership, personal organization, nonprofit general, and sector specific. This simple filing system will make a future review and deeper study more efficient. You may wish to tag video and audio content, which then allows you to consume the content in different settings, such as podcast listening while taking a walk or during your commute.

- **Weekly study**. While your daily review and capture will help further curate the knowledge available to you, the real discipline comes in carving out time in your calendar to actually absorb the content you have saved and begin to consider its practical application. I suggest a (minimally) weekly regimen of distraction-free reading or listening time. Depending on your energy levels, this might be early or late but likely outside of your normal work hours to reduce distraction. Find a quiet time to reflect on the material and (ideally) take notes to encourage the genuine transfer of knowledge from passive listening or reading to active learning. My standard note-taking routine is to capture at least three takeaways from each article, podcast, or information piece. This alone requires more than just a cursory review but is worth the effort since I have already reviewed the content in my initial capture and determined there is value. In most cases, your three takeaways may be the extent of your study on any particular information source, and that may lead to handwritten notes that go along with the source material in a cloud-based filing system such as Evernote. Generally speaking, you may capture one or two items a day, thus leaving you with ten to twelve items for you to process each week. This deeper study should take two or three hours a week, likely through daily reading and listening, when your mental energy is sufficient or perhaps reserved for a quiet weekend block of time.

- **Monthly application.** Curating knowledge in and of itself is not enough. The ultimate objective is to create a system that ensures that you are capturing relevant knowledge for your professional success, spending the time necessary to truly understand it, and, finally, finding ways to apply it to your leadership practice. The funnel effect of these three steps allows you to capture relevant information and then narrow your focus on items of interest, further highlighting those items that can be implemented in a tangible way into your work, your network, or a content piece. To help you assimilate this knowledge, a monthly review might further determine three or four items that you could apply in one of three ways:

  1. **Apply it to your work.** If an idea or concept can help you immediately, consider how you can best share it with your supervisor or colleagues to stimulate their thinking about the topic. Perhaps it is something you can share at the next staff meeting or with a board committee, if not the full

board. The exercise of translating your content piece into a practical application for others will both accelerate your learning and provide practice of a leadership skill that will serve you well as you advance on the path.

2. **Apply it to your network.** Another way to increase your own transfer of knowledge is to "teach" it to someone else. Share the information or content piece with a colleague, mentor, or friend. Make a case for its value, and seek a conversation to discuss it further. By creating an active engagement on the topic, you will be forced to learn more thoroughly, and the additional perspective of your colleague will likely add even more depth to your understanding and strengthen your network at the same time.

3. **Create a content piece.** A final way to truly engage a piece of curated knowledge is to create a piece of content based on the information you have gathered. Examples include the following:

   □ Write a response to the author of the original work, and demonstrate an understanding of the material and how it can be applied to your work.

   □ Write an article yourself on the topic, including a review of the original piece or offering a new take on the topic entirely.

   □ Incorporate, with proper acknowledgment, the content into an existing or forthcoming presentation.

   □ Write a report or reflection memo on the original content piece, even if only for your reference in the future or as a tool for sharing and discussion with colleagues.

Curating knowledge has enormous value as a means to accelerate your learning as well as a method to sharpen skills where you may be deficient. The applications of your newly acquired knowledge not only help to ensure lifelong learning but improve your network at the same time.

With increasing knowledge in all areas of leadership, you are primed to move to the next step on the path, which is to "express yourself" and master the specific forms of communication that allow you to tell your story, to lead effectively, and to make a case for senior leadership.

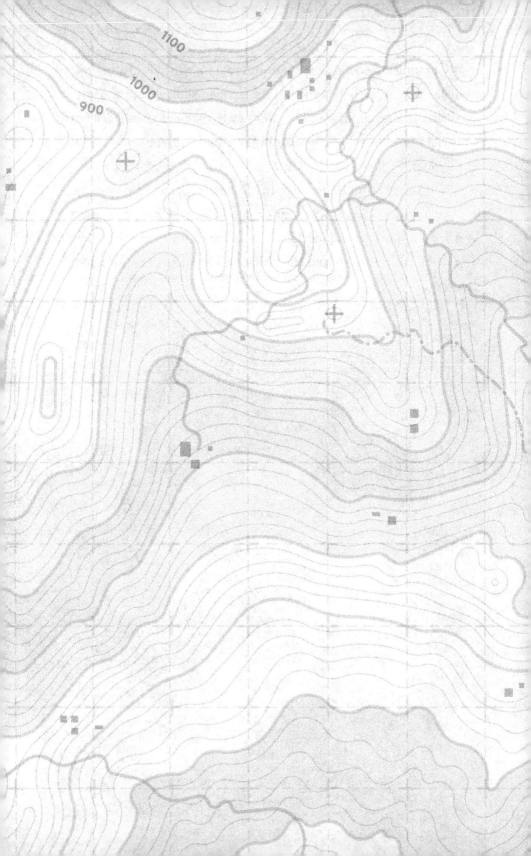

CHAPTER 6

Express Yourself

Having been through the planning phase on the path (Sharpen Your Vision, Map Your Course) and the preparation phase (Get in Shape, Curate Knowledge), it is now time to begin the final phase of building your leadership plan. In this phase, the focus is on implementing skills and engaging external networks that can help you to secure your ideal leadership position and succeed once you arrive.

This chapter focuses on the array of communication skills that you will need to utilize as a nonprofit leader to "express yourself." Though these written and spoken skills will be familiar, this chapter explores each skill, so you understand how each is uniquely important to your nonprofit leadership. The reality is that you may be called upon to design and implement *all* of these forms of communication, and the more comfortable with and effective you are in each medium, the better. Express Yourself will help you to excel at three basic categories of skill:

- Written communication (business memo, persuasive, personal note)

- Spoken communication (formal, impromptu, meeting)

- Presentations (interview, special event)

Written Communication

As a leader, you will often be called upon to design and deliver effective written communication. By understanding the types of written communication you will be expected to utilize, you can begin practicing these formats in your current role:

- Business memo: You will often be called upon to synthesize and summarize issues, particularly for your board of directors.

- Call to action / appeal letter: As the primary spokesperson for your nonprofit, the organization will need your "voice" to articulate the vision and the ways in which key constituents and donors can help.

- Personal notes: Never underestimate the power of a handwritten note. Given the flurry of electronic communications in everyone's lives, a well-timed thank-you to a donor, a note of encouragement to a team member, or a note of congratulations to a professional colleague can have a lasting effect.

Each of these written formats has a distinct purpose and is critical, as they illustrate your management style to internal audiences and key stakeholders and serve to acknowledge and inspire those whose support is essential to your nonprofit's success.

Consider opportunities you have where you can use each of these writing formats, even if it is not required. A business memo is a good format to use the next time you meet with your supervisor and want to provide an update on where you stand on the project as it relates to your annual goals. Learn to be succinct and focused while conveying important information. Practice making your case and illustrating the value of the organization and the impact it has on the community. Fine-tune your presentation until it says exactly what you want to say. If it is awkward or wordy, refine it until it is honed and polished. Finally, there is *always* a value in a handwritten note. Jot a personal note of thanks to a mentor who spent time with you, or to congratulate a colleague who accepted a new job, or to someone who gave generously to your nonprofit. You can seldom thank someone too much, and handwritten notes stand out among the onslaught of electronic communications. Keep it simple but heartfelt. No need for flowery verse; just speak from the heart.

> You can seldom thank someone too much, and handwritten notes stand out among the onslaught of electronic communications.

Spoken Communication

As a nonprofit leader, you will have multiple opportunities to utilize your spoken communication skills in both formal and informal settings. Consider your current approach in each of the settings that follow with regard to how you would assess your current abilities and how you can improve.

FORMAL SPEAKING

This is the classic podium-style presentation that will be part of every nonprofit leader's experience, whether it involves serving as the emcee at your annual awards dinner or leading a presentation at your sector's annual conference. These opportunities are a great way to inform and inspire internal and external audiences about your leadership and the mission of your nonprofit. Allay any fears you have about public speaking with the knowledge that your audience *wants* you to succeed, and remember that they are eager to hear about the cause you represent. Consider three strategic headlines that illustrate your organization's opportunity to thrive. Every formal or keynote presentation affords you an opportunity to share these, and practice brings confidence to your delivery, as well as comfort in knowing you have a framework to respond to any request to speak.

To best frame your formal presentation design, consider a compelling vision based on three components of your nonprofit's mission and vision:

- Describe your mission in tangible ways through descriptive activities and numbers that illustrate impact. *What* exactly do you do—your organization's mission—and *why* are you proud of its accomplishments?

- While acknowledging pride in your nonprofit's accomplishments, make clear that there are many more people to serve or challenges to address. There is still much work to be done. Quantify the number of unserved individuals that you are still hoping to reach or the opportunities that still exist for your nonprofit to make a positive impact.

- "Plant a flag" on a future goal and repeat in every presentation. "We are proud of what we have accomplished as a nonprofit but know there is still much work to do. Three years from now, we plan to double our impact/numbers with your help."

By maintaining this vision framework, you will not only be a more comfortable public speaker, but you will also provide a consistent message that your staff and key volunteers can share at every opportunity, with repeated impact.

IMPROMPTU SPEAKING

As the leader of a nonprofit organization, you will be called upon to address groups large and small on behalf of the organization, often with little or no notice. These occasions not only provide an opportunity to display your public speaking skills but are also opportunities to advance the organization through effective communication and personal interactions. Always be ready to speak! Know your talking points by heart. Be ready to deliver them clearly and succinctly, seemingly off the cuff. Preparation is everything. Some considerations and preparations that can guide you in advance of an impromptu speaking opportunity:

- Begin with gratitude. You can never overthank any group associated with your nonprofit. I always preface any remarks with gratitude for past, present, or future support, whether it be an internal staff audience, a group of volunteers, or simply visitors on a tour of the facility. A built-in gratitude message also allows you time to collect your thoughts and frame any additional comments. Again, speak from the heart. Be genuine.

- Reinforce your mission/vision/action talking points. While you must adapt to the circumstance and gauge whether you have two minutes or twenty, there is always time to reinforce your key messages about your nonprofit. You are proud of the **mission** and can note a specific detail about what has been accomplished and a brief note about the history or founding of your nonprofit. You are motivated by a **vision** of future success based on specific **action steps** that allow anyone who wants to support the organization to do so. This framework will serve you well in the design of a formal presentation but is also a ready-made set of remarks if you are called upon with little or no notice. Focused. Pithy. Effective. Those are your goals.

- Create dialogue. An impromptu setting often provides an opportunity for conversation. While you must be ready with your organizational remarks, as you speak, find out what brought your audience to your nonprofit in the first place or why they are interested in learning more. Find out what they already know by calling on a select few individuals or seeking feedback from the group in general. Ideally, you will discover questions to which you can respond more thoroughly or identify topics about which you can get more information and follow up. (Always look for opportunities to follow up, as you do not want this impromptu dialogue to be the last exchange between this audience and you or your nonprofit.) You can make a lasting impression—and create a fan for life— by going the extra mile and following up with an individual's request for more information from impromptu gatherings such as these.

MEETING SKILLS

For most people, meetings are simply a required attendance on their calendar and an occasional opportunity to chime in if the topic is relevant or the agenda requires a contribution. As an aspiring nonprofit leader, however, you must not underestimate any type of meeting as an opportunity to demonstrate your insight, enthusiasm, and ability to articulate clear messages. You may not lead meetings yet, but you can certainly make a good impression and demonstrate your communication skills on a regular basis, and often staff and board leaders will pay close attention to your succinct and effective remarks. Here are three ways you can take advantage of meetings to practice communication and demonstrate skill without grabbing the limelight or speaking out of turn:

> You must not underestimate any type of meeting as an opportunity to demonstrate your insight, enthusiasm, and ability to articulate clear messages.

- **Always be prepared**. It is easy to dismiss the need to prepare for the regular staff meeting or even committee meetings with board members, given the amount of work on your plate at any given time and your likely ability to "wing it" once you get there. However, you should not underestimate *any* meeting setting as a chance to demonstrate your current leadership skills and future potential. Review each agenda and consider where you can add value, and bring information or prepare notes to supplement your remarks.

- **Lift up other people**. No one likes a meeting participant who only brags about their own accomplishments or whines about their own problems. Think about a soft-spoken colleague in each meeting who deserves recognition and would appreciate your calling attention to their good work. This kind of public gratitude will not go unnoticed by others in the meeting as well. Again, sincerity is crucial. Simple, not grandiose.

- **Organize your thoughts before speaking**. No one wants to hear someone ramble in a meeting or literally collect their thoughts by thinking out loud. Eunice Kennedy Shriver was known to interrupt someone rambling in a meeting with an abrupt, "What is your point?" When I was a young professional, this was a clear reminder to me that a concise and relevant response on any meeting topic would not only avoid her irritation but also provide a framework for meeting responses that could impress other leaders around the table. *Plan and then speak.*

I quickly saw the most effective and impressive meeting participants were thoughtful but *organized* in their meeting responses and presented their ideas in much the same way as they would write an effective business memo. The first statement out of their mouth was a headline with a clear point—for example, "I think Special Olympics should invest in the sport of tennis because of its appeal to an older athlete population." Make your point, and make it immediately clear where you stand. Then verbalize the outline for your supporting points. "There are three reasons I believe this will help us achieve our organizational goals for the year." Then provide your three verbal "bullet points" to reinforce your opening statement. Without rambling, return to your opening statement and restate your thesis. I cannot overstate how this ability—a skill you can practice—can make a positive impression on the leaders in your organization, especially busy board members who gravitate to individuals who can articulate key issues clearly and concisely.

Of course, not every meeting will provide a dramatic audition in front of the founder of your nonprofit, but think about the last few leadership meetings you attended. Could you have been better prepared and added more value? When you did speak, did you organize your thoughts with a clear thesis and supporting points? Do not miss opportunities to practice effective communication, as you will eventually be modeling this behavior as you lead these meetings yourself.

Presentation Skills

As a nonprofit leader, you will be asked to combine your formal—and sometimes informal—speaking and communication skills in a large-group setting that will allow you to shine. The first "presentation" to consider is an interview for your next nonprofit leadership opportunity, and the second is a presentation for your nonprofit as part of an annual meeting or gala, or perhaps to a state or national conference.

INTERVIEW

Before you have the opportunity to practice nonprofit leadership, you will likely go through the traditional rituals associated with a job search, including an interview. I hope the tenets of this book provide you a baseline of information and preparation that will be beneficial for that process, and it is not too early to consider the content and approach you will take when given such an opportunity. The formal interview with a hiring nonprofit (and the informal introductions to board members and staff) provides you a perfect chance to share your personal case for support and articulate your vision for nonprofit leadership.

- **Know your audience**. If this is an organization you have targeted as an ideal fit for your leadership aspirations, then you are likely familiar with their staff leadership. Find out as much as you can about the makeup of the search committee and who exactly will be leading the efforts to review candidates. If the organization has employed a search firm or recruiter to help with their efforts, that person should be able to illuminate much of the process and exactly who will be involved.

- **Study the organization**. Know it in depth. Your level of knowledge will indicate your level of interest.

- **Match your experience to the job description**. The job description is a quick statement of need; show how you answer that need.

- **Anticipate the leadership questions**. What more might they want to know about you? How might they try to place value on what you have to offer?

PRESENTATIONS

Given the requirement that nonprofit leaders will have to address both internal and external audiences on multiple occasions, it pays to consider your approach to the necessary preparation and delivery.

- Know your audience. Speak directly to their needs.

- Determine the format, previous presentations, others on the agenda. Match your presentation to their interests.

- Imagine the takeaways for yourself and for your audience. What will they be hoping for from the meeting?

- Manage your technology. Always test your technology before the presentation. Nothing says "unprepared" like technology snafus.

- Focus on the opening and the conclusion. Grab your audience at the get-go, and end by giving them the sense that they are glad they heard you.

By focusing on these key communication skills, you will better prepare for your first nonprofit leadership opportunity as well as maintain leadership roles once you are established. While these skills might be familiar, do not underestimate how important they are.

Communication is easy if you prepare and if you focus on honing your speech to be concise and informative. Simple is always best. Be ready when you are called upon to design and implement *all* of these forms of communication, and *Expressing Yourself* will be an area in which you can excel. Now we can turn our attention to the next stop on the path, "Building Community."

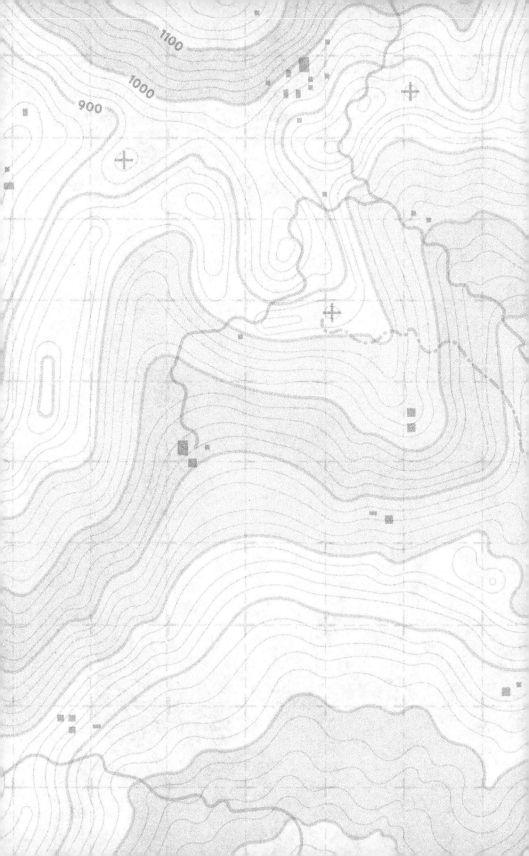

CHAPTER 7

Build Community

As you organize your plan for senior leadership in the nonprofit sector, you have assessed and improved individual skills that will prepare you for the journey. The most successful leaders, however, move beyond their individual attributes and activities—to utilize the vast resources available to them within their personal and professional networks. Just as you considered the various communication skills you will utilize in the previous chapter, this chapter will continue the implementation phase of the path.

By building community, you will create a framework to maximize your internal and external networks, as well as find ways to expand these networks in ways that are mutually beneficial for both you and your new connections.

This effort is not about expanding your network through vanity metrics, such as social media followers and likes, nor is it about attending endless networking events and socials. Your digital presence and appropriate attendance have their place, but this chapter is about a strategic approach to networking and building a community based on mutual recognition and support. This is about developing meaningful relationships that you can maintain through professional transitions and relocations, identifying colleagues who can hold you accountable to your own goals and aspirations, and also offer encouragement as you face inevitable challenges and disappointments.

As such, there are three elements to help you **build community**:

- Targeted networking

- Two-way coaching and mentoring

- A personal board of directors

Targeted Networking

For some, the term *networking* often suggests attending receptions during your annual conference and going early to your local National Philanthropy Day event or Chamber of Commerce social. While these "networking" activities are fine, the best networking will actually occur when you are more intentional about who you want to connect with. Instead of just going to the reception or networking event and waiting to meet someone, *invite* your networking target to meet you there.

Who might be a "networking target"? This is a person who will have overlapping interests and professional aspirations and can benefit from your experience just as much as you can from theirs. I suggest you consider two categories of networking targets: **comparison colleagues** and **aspirational colleagues**.

COMPARISON COLLEAGUE

A *comparison colleague* is in a similar role to yours, likely having been in the nonprofit sector for a comparable timeframe as well. To deepen your understanding of the sector in which you work, first look at other organizations in your community that serve a similar mission, and look at the staff directory of the other organizations to determine who has the same or equivalent role to yours. There is certainly value in identifying comparison colleagues in other nonprofit sectors as well.

Use this exercise to identify five or six comparison colleagues from their website bios or LinkedIn profiles, and request a networking call or video conference. Make it clear that you are impressed with their career progress and that you would like to ask some questions about their work and professional path. Ideally, your potential colleague will agree to what amounts to a no-obligation call or meeting. Suggest forty-five minutes for the initial conversation, and if it goes well, you can certainly invite further discussion. Consider four basic topics in this type of networking call:

- Why did you get into nonprofit work, and what led to your current position?

- What accomplishment are you most proud of since arriving at your current role?

- What has been your biggest challenge since you arrived?

- What resources and advice have been most helpful during your career so far?

These four questions, especially if they are reciprocated, will easily consume a forty-five-minute meeting. The design of the "interview" puts the spotlight on your new colleague and gives them the chance to share the wisdom of their professional experience, which most people are honored to do. If you and your potential comparisons colleague do not "hit it off," there is certainly no harm done. You have still learned about a similar nonprofit professional and gained insight into another organization that you can file away for future reference. Thank them for their time with a follow-up email or handwritten note (with your business card enclosed) and offer yourself as a resource in the future.

ASPIRATIONAL COLLEAGUE

The pursuit of an *aspirational colleague* is similar. Begin with researching individuals who serve in a role that you hope to attain or look for organizations that are further along in their growth and maturity than yours. Ideally, the individual you seek is someone who can offer value based on their additional leadership experiences and also provide insight on their nonprofit's growth and development, which gives you a glimpse of what success might look like for your organization in five to ten years.

Aspirational colleagues (and organizations) are usually not difficult to identify, especially if you are intentional during any community conversation by asking: "Who is considered the best in our sector at doing the job I do?" or "Which organization in our sector is considered the best in class?" Another way to answer those questions is to review award winners at your recent sector-specific state and national conferences, which often lift up both individual and organizational accolades on a regular basis.

These best-in-class individuals are likely busy but are not impossible to reach. You may find a mutual connection who could introduce you, but a direct approach is not out of the question either. The fact is, flattery works, and most of us are proud of our accomplishments and happy to share. Once again, a structured set of questions—such as those offered to your comparison colleague—should work fine and should give you great insight and ideas to bolster your career development plan.

I suggest a handwritten note (again, with your business card enclosed) as the best means to leave a lasting and positive impression. If the discussion generated any action items (an offer to help you connect with someone else or share a particular resource), mention that in your follow-up, but be careful about "abusing" the introductory call by asking for additional favors. Make a note of the topics discussed, especially ones that will help you identify an appropriate follow-up in the future, such as a career milestone or an organizational anniversary.

The beauty of this strategic networking activity is that you develop a powerful community in a relatively short period of time. Imagine how quickly your network can expand if you simply schedule one comparison colleague call and one aspirational colleague call each month. Finally, this effort to build community also provides the network from which you will develop other support structures detailed in this chapter, including coaching and mentor relationships and your personal board of directors.

Two-Way Coaching

While targeted networking activities will help you to identify and build an invaluable community, the exchanges are largely informational. The next element of **building community** is to find connections that move beyond information and resource exchange and help you to incorporate accountability as well as the opportunity to develop the talents of others.

Coaching relationships often occur in an informal manner within the nonprofit community, but there is increasing recognition of the value of formal (paid) coaching arrangements as well as more intentional mentoring partnerships. The cost has often made coaching seem like a luxury many nonprofits could not afford, but boards of directors are starting to realize that this kind of professional development for their senior leaders is well worth the investment and significantly less than the cost of burnout and turnover.

This heightened appreciation for coaching in the nonprofit sector may not trickle down to your current position at the organization, but it is worth discussing with your supervisor what possibilities exist for professional development funds (if they exist at all). Your interest in leadership coaching should be viewed as a proactive sign that you want to be more productive in the role you are in now, as well as prepare you for greater responsibilities down the road. Fortunately, more nonprofit managers are recognizing the value of professional development as a means to retain their best talent versus a defensive posture that assumes you will develop your skills and simply leave. It is hard to understand this logic since organizations that do not invest in their future leaders are certain to lose them anyway!

> This kind of professional development for their senior leaders is well worth the investment and significantly less than the cost of burnout and turnover.

If your organization does not have the ability to support leadership coaching for you, it may be worth exploring that investment on your own. Two potential avenues include full-time coaches and sector-specific consultants and internal arrangements.

FULL-TIME AND SECTOR-SPECIFIC PROFESSIONAL COACHES

Costs and plans vary widely, but it will not hurt to evaluate coaches in your community (or those increasingly available online if you are comfortable with a virtual or phone experience). Coaches of this kind should have evidence of certifications and training and can clearly define their role as a coach, versus simply someone who provides encouragement. A good coach should identify mutually agreed-upon goals, help you to detail a plan, and then hold you accountable for progress. These consultants sometimes offer discounted rates for non-profits as well. Nonprofit consulting firms such as mine offer coaching services as part of larger engagements with nonprofits (e.g., work with fundraising staff on a campaign or with the executive director as part of a strategic planning process). I also offer individual and group consulting programs, like the Mastermind Program that is described in chapter 9, "Resources and Next Steps." It is also worth exploring other resources through the local and state-level associations of which your nonprofit is a member. Ask around to see if others in your sector have used and can recommend coaching resources.

INFORMAL COACHING ARRANGEMENTS

Coaching does not have to be a formal arrangement or a paid service. You could simply identify a friend or colleague and ask them to be an "accountability partner," agreeing to share each other's professional goals for a defined period of time (perhaps six months). You could commit to a frequency of meetings and a format in which each of you shares progress at those meetings and offer advice and encouragement when progress is not being made. While you and your partner may lack the skills and training that a professional coach would bring, you are certainly better off than most. Another resource to investigate might be coaching certification programs in your community, as their participants may need coaching clients with whom they can train. While they lack experience, they do bring formal training, and a month or two of work with them may offer new accountability, insight, and encouragement for your professional plan.

You are wise to explore leadership coaching during your journey on the path to nonprofit leadership, but continue to do so after you have "arrived" at the senior position you hope to obtain. Nonprofit leadership is a dynamic exercise and will require ongoing self-evaluation, reflection, and accountability to goals that move you and your organization forward. Your continuing use of professional coaching also sets an important example for those who work with and for you. Just as you recognize the value that coaching has for you, you will be an increasingly important coach for those who report to you, as well as for those who look up to you throughout the organization, such as volunteers, board members, or employees.

Anticipating the importance of your role as a coach through your nonprofit leadership, it is necessary that you seek opportunities to coach others so that you can develop that important leadership skill. As discussed, this might take the form of an accountability partner with whom you share goals, plans, and progress. While the earlier reference was to emphasize the value of coaching for you, this emphasis is to focus on the delivery of good coaching to *someone else*. By seeking someone else you can help as a coach, you can focus on three things:

> It is necessary that you seek opportunities to coach others so that you can develop that important leadership skill.

- *The importance of critical listening and conversational skills.* What are this person's actual goals? Why do they aspire to the goals they share? What challenges have they identified that currently inhibit their progress? Are you able to ask good questions that help someone better articulate their professional situation?

- *The importance of measurable goals.* Having listened to their long-term objectives, can you help them to develop the specific, measurable, actionable, relevant, and time-based (SMART) goals they need? Coaching will allow you to practice the skill of turning professional evaluations into activities that help someone improve, a skill that will be formalized as you actually manage an increasing number of professionals as your leadership roles expand.

- *The importance of accountability.* Just as you seek coaching to hold yourself accountable to the ambitious goals you are setting, so your ability to coach others in that way is equally important. By encouraging actionable goals, you help them set a timeline by which these goals must be accomplished. You also help them evaluate their current routines and rituals that either enhance or impede their progress. It is not always easy to hold someone accountable, but your ability to practice a supportive yet realistic appraisal of their progress is a skill that will transfer directly to your leadership of individuals reporting to you as a nonprofit leader.

Personal Board of Directors

As you develop your network through targeted contacts and build deeper professional relationships through coaching and mentors, an additional support mechanism to consider is the establishment of a **personal board of directors**. Just as you look at your nonprofit's board as a critical resource to the advancement of the organization's mission, so you can also personally benefit from a similar group to help you advance on your path to nonprofit leadership.

The questions to consider as you build your personal board are similar to the nomination process that your nonprofit uses as it seeks new members. You want a diverse set of skills and experiences from a group of people who believe in your mission and want to help you to succeed. Personally, I have benefited from this concept for more than fifteen years, and it has allowed me the opportunity to engage highly talented individuals during different stages of my career.

The idea is not necessarily to create the administrative infrastructure that an organization's board requires. The group is more akin to a virtual advisory panel that can individually, and sometimes collectively, support you on specific elements of your career journey. I have never assembled my personal board together at one time but have mentioned the presence of other members to illustrate the concept and to reinforce to each individual the unique characteristics they bring and the value for which I am grateful.

As you contemplate this concept, it is helpful to think of yourself just as you would a start-up nonprofit organization. In creating a board for a start-up, you would naturally look for a variety of skills and experiences to build an advisory group that could advise the founder on the different types of issues they would face. As you are the "founder" of your personal organization, here are the types of individuals whom I would seek in the formation of a seven-member personal board of directors:

- *A Comparable Peer within Your Sector.* This person becomes another set of eyes and ears for you in the sector in which you both are working but is removed from the immediate environment of your current employer.

- *A Comparable Peer outside Your Sector.* While sector-specific insight is important to have on your board, someone outside your sector can also add value. This person can become an even greater asset if they are selected from a sector that is of interest to you.

- *Aspirational Leader in Your Sector.* Like the comparable peer in your sector, you want someone who knows the dynamics of organizations like yours, is well connected, and would enjoy a coaching or mentoring-type arrangement.

- *Aspirational Leader outside Your Community.* If you are open to moving to another community, or in fact, *want* to explore another community, then you would be wise to identify a board member who is well established as an executive director there and could advise you about key trends as well as identify opportunities that emerge down the road.

- *A Nonprofit Board Leader.* Given the importance of board relations to your senior leadership success, it is good to have someone on your board who is serving as a nonprofit board member outside of your current nonprofit. You can decide if you want to maintain a very sector-focused board based on your certainty of remaining in it on your path to senior leadership.

- *Nonprofit Subject-Matter Expert.* There are five leadership elements that are always part of senior leadership positions in the nonprofit sector: strategic planning, board development, staff development, fundraising, and finance and budgeting. The board member identified for the previous position of your board will help to ensure that you have board development covered, so the other four areas are worth considering as you target personal board candidates.

- *Personal Subject-Matter Expert.* As you advance on your nonprofit leadership journey, your need for good legal and financial management advice will increase. This personal board member can be someone with the expertise to help you to evaluate an employment contract you are considering or help you to evaluate the types of legal issues you may encounter in your future leadership role. An additional board member may be someone in the financial services area who can help you to evaluate the different aspects of not just compensation but also retirement funds, insurance, and other benefits that will affect you and your family.

Now that you have considered the ideal combination of skills and experiences that you would like to have on your board, here are the steps to consider so that you can make the group operational and the kind of resource you need them to be.

- Clarify your expectations and how the group will be organized. The fact is that while the group brings a significant amount of collective wisdom, it is not necessary for them to ever assemble together. The group dynamic will be apparent to you, but each of them likely only has a relationship with you alone. There may be an occasion when you intentionally connect two or more of your board members when you feel it is mutually beneficial, but there is no requirement to do so.

- Create a nominating matrix document that allows you to look at each of your board candidates and the attributes they bring to the relationship with you. While the primary seven attributes you are seeking were defined previously, you will also want to cross-reference secondary attributes that add other perspectives as well. For example, your attorney friend on the board may also be from a community in which you have an interest, or perhaps your nonprofit subject-matter expert in strategic planning may also work in a different nonprofit sector in which you have an interest.

- Before you approach any of your board candidates, practice your vision framework, as discussed previously in chapter 3, "Sharpen Your Vision." As each candidate considers whether they can help you in this advisory manner, you must clarify why their help will be essential to your achieving leadership success in the nonprofit sector. They will want to know what timeline you are on and where you stand on vision framework questions such as geography, sector, and the type of organization you want to lead. Of course, they will also want to know exactly how you want them to help.

In defining the role you want them to play, share the concept of your personal board with them, and let them know the expertise and experience you have identified that is unique to them and why it will be invaluable to your success. Confirm that you would like them to serve for a two-year period and that you will reach out no more than two or three times a year.

Note that you will set these meetings at their convenience and will create a discussion outline each time. Suggest that you are seeking their advice on the types of information you need to learn in their area and where you might find the tools and resources necessary to acquire the requisite skills and knowledge. Indicate that you would welcome their advice on a timeline of activity that would assure progress over a two-year period and that you would appreciate their help in holding you accountable and assessing your progress.

- Provide regular (quarterly) communication to each member of your board, simply providing professional updates and encouraging their input on any general trends they are seeing and on any specific items related to the specific topics about which you two have discussed.

- The only reward a personal board member will likely require is to see your progress toward your nonprofit leadership goal. If you have cultivated them successfully, then you have already found common ground before discussing the personal board concept at all, and they will likely find it personally and professionally rewarding to stay connected to you and your various nonprofit associations. Be sure to repeatedly express your appreciation to each member, and be respectful of their time and provide a clear outline before and after each meeting or conversation. While they understand the association is about supporting you, make sure you look for ways to add value for *them* as well. The point is, treat them with the same courtesy and respect that you would show a member of your organization's board of directors. As a result, you will find this personal board structure an invaluable way to accelerate your journey on the path.

As you can see from the focus given to building community in this chapter, I am a strong believer in the power of strategic networking. The "build community" mindset will help you to see connections and future opportunities with nearly every professional contact you make. Some may simply serve as a one-time networking call and help you to gather intelligence on a sector, community, or topic. Others may become a coaching connection, providing you with the accountability you seek to keep your plan in motion or perhaps providing *you* the chance to coach and strengthen your personnel management skills. A select few may rise to the level of serving on your personal board of directors and be part of a powerful collective that helps you on your path to nonprofit leadership for years to come. Empowered by a strong community of support, you are now ready to "practice leadership."

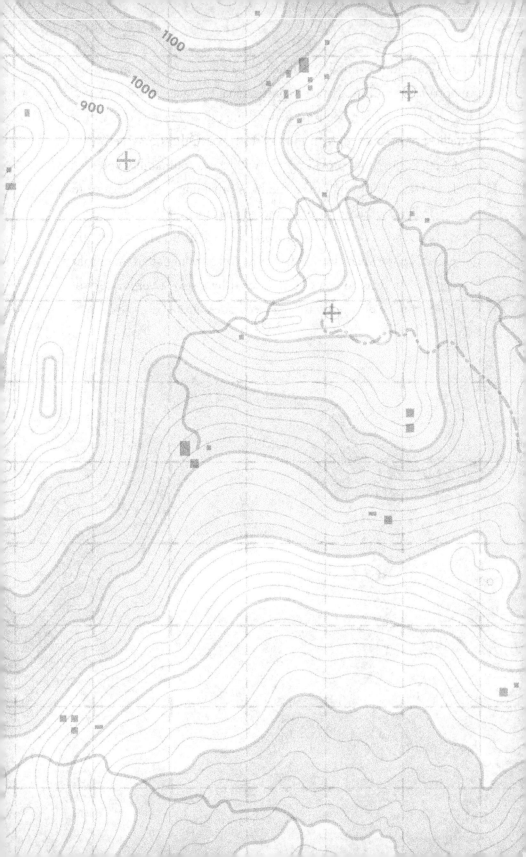

CHAPTER 8

Practice Leadership

N ow that you have contemplated each of the components on the path through the planning and preparation phases as defined in previous chapters, it is time to ensure that you can implement them and find ways to practice the skills that will be crucial to your successfully obtaining the nonprofit leadership role you desire. The fact is, there are many ways to practice leadership regardless of the formal authority you have in your current role, but you will need to be intentional about finding these opportunities so that you can be better prepared to respond to likely interview questions for future job opportunities.

This chapter will help you to identify each of the elements of leadership in which you must be proficient and, more importantly, find ways to practice these important skills. The chapter is organized into six sections:

- Strategic planning
- Implementation

- Board development

- Staff development

- Fundraising

- Budgeting and finance

While actual job descriptions will vary (as you know from your study of aspirational job descriptions in chapter 5, "Curate Knowledge"), senior roles within the nonprofit sector will always include these five leadership components. As you evaluate the skills and experiences required to advance your career, consider the depth of your knowledge in each of these areas, as well as what opportunities you have to practice that knowledge. While there are substantial texts on each of these topics, the purpose of this chapter is to orient you at a high level and offer additional resources on the book's online resource page.

Strategic Planning

As discussed in your individual assessment as part of chapter 4, "Mapping Your Course," strategic planning is a skill and experience you will require to demonstrate proficiency before leading a nonprofit organization. While there are volumes of texts exploring the concept of strategy for any type of organization (and I have offered reference material in the resources section on each of these five topics), I find it helpful to articulate strategy in four distinct areas:

SETTING THE VISION

As a nonprofit leader, you must help the organization to imagine a future state that drives all other planning activities in an effort to achieve this future. While the organization's dream vision may be the eradication of the challenge it faces (e.g., curing cancer, ending homelessness, grade-level reading proficiency for all third graders), a strategic planning vision should be targeted at a ten-year horizon that allows for a bold but attainable goal orientation.

ASSESSING THE ORGANIZATION

As part of a strategic planning process, or even as part of your arrival to a new organization as its leader, you will be asked to conduct an organizational assessment. As with the process for setting the vision, you may want to utilize outside counsel for facilitation to assure a neutral third-party review, especially since some of the findings may be sensitive for staff and/or the board. In general, this assessment should identify and evaluate categories of data about the nonprofit.

> A strategic planning vision should be targeted at a ten-year horizon that allows for a bold but attainable goal orientation.

- The first is its internal strengths, and specifically, how these strengths can be better utilized or maximized to the organization's greater advantage.

- The second area of an assessment is the nonprofit's greatest internal weaknesses or challenges.

- Again, a good assessment does not simply provide a list of these challenges but prioritizes them in terms of urgency to address.

- The third assessment area moves to an external review and illuminates opportunities and threats. Opportunities often appear when the organization looks at other nonprofits serving the same population or embracing a similar mission, and the possibility of partnerships or alliances shines through. While external threats are difficult to predict (economic conditions, a global pandemic), the organization must still consider what contingency plans it will employ if an unforeseen threat becomes a reality.

PRIORITIZATIONS AND GOAL SETTING

Once the ten-year vision is clear and the organizational assessment provides clarity of the nonprofit's current start, it is time to build the plan through goal-setting and prioritized activity. Your job will be to demonstrate an ability to grasp the conclusions from the assessments and do something about them! When I am working with a nonprofit on their strategic plan, I translate each of the categories from the assessment into action items in the following way.

For strengths, first look for the top-three organizational attributes and prioritize them by determining which three strengths can be built upon to help the organization move closer to its ten-year vision.

- For example, if tests are showing that the after-school tutoring program is the most effective among all of the tutoring programs in the community, then increasing the capacity of this program—an existing strength—could become a clear goal for the next year. This accomplishes both the prioritizing exercise—*What is our top-performing program?*—and leverages it in a mission-enhancing way. To complete the exercise, a specific goal should be established by putting one-, three-, and five-year growth plans in place to double the capacity of the program in five years. Your ability to articulate a prioritization and goal-setting exercise demonstrates a clear understanding of this phase of strategic planning and moves the process closer to implementation, the "bias for action" that nonprofit organizations are looking for when they hire leaders.

Prioritization and goal setting can be illustrated in each of the other three assessment areas. Just as you identified a key strength and prioritized it among all of the others and set a goal accordingly, the same can be done from reviewing the organization's weaknesses and challenges. While the assessment may have revealed ten to twelve weaknesses or areas in need of improvement, you must decide which one or two should be addressed first to have the most positive impact on the organization. Nonprofit organizations cannot address every weakness at once, and the importance of prioritization is quite clear given that reality.

- Perhaps the same after-school tutoring program mentioned had determined that significant challenges were the cumbersome paperwork required to enroll a new student and the inefficiency of actual paper forms that captured information and then had to be entered into the organization's computer system. This weakness certainly creates a barrier to enrollment growth and also stresses the capacity of the staff, given the time required to enter data. A resulting goal, therefore, could be the development of an online registration portal in the next year that would offer greater accessibility, ease of data entry, and a reduction of redundant staff time.

As an aspiring nonprofit leader, consider similar examples you have seen within your own organization that you could share in a conversation with an aspirational colleague or in an interview for a new job. The same prioritization and goal-setting process can be applied to external opportunities and threats, as well. What single opportunity shows the most promise and should be explored first? What threat is most likely and, therefore, what contingency plan should be put in place this year?

Now that you have a clearer understanding of the elements of an assessment and how to turn them into action, you are ready to tackle the final element of good strategic planning: implementation.

Implementation

Strategic plans are only as good as the results they produce. You can set the vision, assess the organization, and prioritize the goals, *but none of that matters if you cannot put the plan into action.* Your understanding of the following four questions regarding implementation will round out your knowledge of strategic planning:

- ***What exactly will success look like for this goal?*** It is one thing to say that the organization will double the number of participants in its after-school tutoring program, but specifi-

> You can set the vision, assess the organization, and prioritize the goals, *but none of that matters if you cannot put the plan into action.*

cally, what is required to achieve that goal? Clearly, it will take more space, more tutors, and more materials, among other things. Each component part must be broken down so that progress toward implementation can be clearly assessed and measured.

- ***What are the resources necessary to accomplish this goal?*** Successful implementation will require an early review of the time required, the budget necessary, and the personnel involved. Inadequate planning for any of these areas will make successful implementation impossible.

- ***Who is responsible for achieving this goal?*** Many organizations have failed in their effort to achieve a strategic planning goal because they did not make sure *one* person was responsible. That does not mean this person must work alone, but successful implementation requires clear accountability and oversight and that it not be left as an "organizational goal" or the responsibility of the "program team." This is vague and offers no accountability.

  - Knowing the person responsible and allowing them to be part of the implementation plan, including defining the exact outcome and the resources necessary, will go a long way to ensuring success.

- ***What is the timeline for this goal to be achieved?*** While you may already have prioritized a goal and created general one-, three-, or five-year time horizons, successful implementation requires a more detailed project timeline or tracker. "Next year" becomes "next September" when the new program begins, and "next September" is the last of a dozen calendar milestones that must be met to ensure success by the target deadline.

Again, this outline simply provides a working knowledge of strategic planning but represents a realistic overview of a process that you should learn more about, find ways to practice, and be prepared to articulate in an interview setting for your ideal nonprofit leadership opportunity.

Board Development

Just as you must understand and articulate your approach to strategic planning, so you will also be expected to understand and articulate a plan for working with your nonprofit board of directors. As in each of these critical leadership knowledge areas, I find it helpful to retain a numeric framework to define a larger approach to the subject area. For strategic planning, there were four elements to understand and explain. For board development, I believe there are also four topics to consider:

- **Board development starts with a clear job description.** Too many nonprofit board members cannot define their board role and either never receive a written expectation of their role or do not adhere to the one they were given. This is problematic for the board member and executive director relationship for sure, and board role clarity should be your first objective in responding to a question about board development. This allows you to articulate the governance function of the board in terms of strategic, fiscal, and legal oversight and also clarifies the limits of board members in day-to-day operations.

- **Distinguish board and staff rules.** Similarly, your approach to board development should be clear on the role of board members in terms of interacting with the staff. Legally, their job is to hire (and occasionally fire) the chief executive. As that chief executive, it is your responsibility to hire and manage everyone else. Problems can occur when board members use their influence to direct the activity of members of your team. It is crucial that you make the distinction clear about appropriate and inappropriate board-staff interactions in early stage conversations between you and your board leadership; ideally, this should be discussed during the interview process.

- **Fundraising expectations.** Similar to the overall issue of board members lacking clarity about their "job description," there is often a potentially awkward expectation around fundraising. I believe that all board members should make an annual personal financial contribution at a level that is meaningful to them; I do not believe in setting a minimum contribution. As the chief executive, you must take the responsibility of encouraging each board member to give at a level commensurate with their financial means and consistent with their commitment to this nonprofit as one of their top-three charitable priorities. Also, it is important that *all* board members contribute to the process of fundraising (and not necessarily the "asking for money" part). The point of this section, however, is that you must be comfortable in your expectations for board giving to and participating in the fundraising process, as it is certain to be a topic of discussion when you explore and interview with a new organization.

- **Nominating philosophy.** A characteristic I look for in excellent nonprofit boards is a proactive and year-round approach to nominating. The best boards are constantly but carefully seeking talent to join their ranks. This includes a philosophy of term limits and not bringing on members who appear to be on the board for life. Evidence of this type of outstanding board would include a chart of the current members, with clearly defined attributes of their diverse demographics, professional skills, geographic and programmatic experience, and interests in committee and overall board leadership. This type of thoughtful approach to board development and recruitment makes it much easier to attract and retain new members, as well. By taking "inventory" of all of the current gaps in skills and experiences needed, the nominating process can become even more strategic with each passing year. As a nonprofit leader, you can look to this nominating philosophy as one you can initiate at your current organization and be prepared to discuss with your future nonprofit as well.

Staff Development

Board development is a critical leadership concept about which you should have knowledge and experience, but equally important is your understanding and approach to staff development. Inherent in every interview process will be a question: "What type of boss will you be?" While your immediate response will likely include some variation of "I am not a micromanager" or "I have an open-door policy," you would be wise to consider a more detailed philosophy and approach about how you will lead the kind of team necessary to succeed. Once again, I suggest you consider a framework of staff development concepts that you could share in an interview environment and, more importantly, implement as a nonprofit leader. Here are four such concepts to consider:

- **Clarity of job descriptions.** Just as your philosophy around board development starts with role clarity, so too should your approach to staff development begin there. Too often, even large and relatively sophisticated nonprofits do not have adequate job descriptions or do not follow them. While the full description is warranted from a human resources perspective, you want to bring a prioritized focus to each of the senior leaders that report to you. What are the three most mission-critical aspects of their job, and what specific accomplishments or metrics would indicate success in the upcoming twelve months? This approach to staff development ensures a bias for strategic action and more efficient use of staff meetings. It also substantiates the cliché about not being a micromanager and allows your team to independently create an annual plan to which you can hold them accountable.

- **Commitment to professional development.** Though every leader says this, you must be prepared to elaborate on what you mean by it. Using your organization's strategic planning acumen, you will use a similar assessment model for your team members. After having your team complete a self-assessment, identify the top one or two strengths on which each team member can build this year and the one or two challenges they can address as well. These professional development goals become part of each member's annual plan and are reviewed with the same importance as their other job description goals as defined in the previous section. This type of intentional goal setting will ensure that your approach to professional development is more than a vague promise and also allows you to consider specific budgetary requests that can support your team leader's efforts to build on their strengths and improve on their weaknesses.

- **Positive reinforcement through accountability.** The nonprofit sector has a justifiable reputation as a feel-good environment in which to work. The mission should be rewarding, and there is a great sense of accomplishment in seeing evidence of your nonprofit's impact. However, a feel-good environment must include accountability, and as a nonprofit leader, you will be expected to hold your staff responsible. An underlying question in an interview is whether you are prepared to make tough decisions as the team leader and even dismiss personnel when necessary. Your quick response will, of course, be "Yes," but give thoughtful consideration to what scenario would warrant a dismissal. By offering the first two elements in this section—clear job descriptions and a commitment to professional development—you demonstrate a leadership style that is based on positive reinforcement. It also adds clarity to each individual's annual expectations and makes it more likely that course corrections can be made and light can be shed on an issue well before it becomes an offense worthy of termination. You owe it to every member of the team, and to the mission of the organization, to expect excellence every day. When that is made very clear, those who cannot perform at the same level should be granted a graceful exit well before a dramatic dismissal is required.

- **Perpetual talent development and internal promotion.** The best way to offer positive reinforcement is to encourage each member of your team to expand on their professional responsibilities and leadership and groom them for every promotion possible. Have conversations with each member of your team about their ultimate nonprofit leadership role. As much as possible, find a path for them within your organization while also acknowledging that they may have to move on to achieve their most senior leadership goals. Rather than be possessive of great team members, your encouragement of their success will create a culture in which others will want to stay the course, even if they lose great opportunities elsewhere. While first focusing your talent development efforts internally, also keep your hand on the pulse of talent outside of your organization. Be on the lookout for up-and-coming nonprofit professionals, and make yourself available as a coach and a mentor. You never know when you will have an opening for a key position (and you will), and your ability to constantly build community will pay off through direct candidate connections and indirect referrals when the time is right.

Fundraising

Every nonprofit leadership discussion or interview soon turns to the topic of fundraising. Your path to nonprofit leadership should include careful study of all aspects of philanthropy and the acquisition of as much experience as possible in the areas of individual, corporate, and foundation fundraising. Once again, this section is designed to give you a high-level overview of the concepts that you should master. Explore many of the countless resources on fundraising that will help you address any questions or topics on which you want more information (see the resources page at www.pattonmcdowell.com). In an interview setting, you will almost certainly have an opportunity to address your "fundraising philosophy" or your approach to fundraising. Consider the following concepts as the basis for an informed discussion on exactly that topic:

- **Know where charitable dollars come from.** Understanding where an organization's current streams of revenue come from should be part of your pre-interview research, but you should also be clear in your understanding of charitable trends, as evidenced by Giving USA's annual report. The great majority (80+ percent) of charitable gifts are made by individuals and families, and while corporate and foundation giving should not be ignored, the majority of a nonprofit's fundraising resources should be devoted to cultivating and stewarding the individuals and families who have the greatest potential to give.

- **Distinguish between the three primary fundraising programs.** Most nonprofits focus their fundraising efforts on annual giving activities: direct mail, online appeals, and special events. While this entry-level giving is important, it is only a part of the comprehensive fundraising program that must be in place. There must also be a major gifts program—which simply means the organization can articulate clear investment opportunities for larger gifts. If annual fund activity encourages giving in amounts from $25 to $1,000, then the major gifts programs should clearly illustrate the value of investments of $5,000 to $1,000,000. Too many nonprofits are stuck in a perpetual grind as they chase the labor-intensive smaller gifts year after year, while not shifting a portion of their time and energy to a smaller group of donor prospects who have the ability to make a five-, six-, or even seven-figure gift. Similarly, the third program that must be in place in a healthy nonprofit fundraising program is a planned giving or legacy program. While difficult to measure given the deferred nature of these gifts, having a legacy program is still a critical part of an organization's philanthropy program because it demonstrates a long-term mindset at the organization and is often the source of the most significant and transformational gifts the nonprofit will receive. Despite the uncertainty and the "wait" for a planned gift to materialize, legacy donors are also often *more* likely to support their designated charity while they are still alive. Your ability to explain and differentiate all three types of fundraising programs will ensure that your current organization remains solvent and shows that you understand the work necessary to achieve short- and long-term investments.

- **Assure a commitment to all five phases of the development cycle.** To best illustrate your understanding of fundraising, make abundantly clear that you know successful philanthropic organizations focus on more than just "asking for money."

    1. While *soliciting funds or inviting investment* is, in fact, one of the five phases of the development cycle, it is not the only one—and not even the first one—on which to focus. A good fundraising organization first seeks to identify and study its most likely donor prospects. You will not have the time or resources to appeal to everyone in your community, which I often describe as "volume fundraising." On the surface, it seems to make sense: "If we can just get ten dollars from each of the thousand letters we mail, we will be fine." This desired result rarely comes true. A better approach is to identify one hundred current or prospective donors who have given before or have given to a similar cause and then appeal to them in a more targeted and personalized way.

    2. The second phase of the development cycle is *communication*. Once you have identified the most likely donors to your cause, you can focus on sharpening a compelling message that both informs them about your organization and also motivates them to give.

    3. Now that we have identified likely targets and articulated a message that encourages their giving, it is time to illuminate

the third phase of the development cycle: *cultivation*. Just because someone has been identified and informed about the cause, that does not mean they are necessarily motivated to make a gift. What can the organization do to bring this prospective donor closer to the mission? Often, this involves a tour of the facility, attending an event that features the work or programming of the nonprofit, or a meeting with someone close to the cause: a client, volunteer, or board member. These events and activities cultivate the donor's interest and educate them about the accomplishments of the nonprofit and ways that their gift can make a significant difference in future accomplishments.

4. It is then and only then that the fourth phase is appropriate: *Asking for the gift*. This action is appropriate after a prospective donor has been identified, informed, and cultivated, and then this phase is less about convincing someone to give and more about facilitating the best method for them to invest.

5. Finally, a strong philanthropic organization never forgets the fifth phase of the development cycle: *donor stewardship*. It is critical that an organization acknowledges donor contributions with authentic gratitude and continues to express appreciation for the ongoing impact that their gift made toward the mission of the nonprofit. Needless to say, an effective donor stewardship program assures that donors remain connected to the organization and, thus, are more likely to give again.

Fundraising is a full-time profession, and you should explore each of the three elements outlined in this section in much greater detail.

As an aspiring nonprofit leader, you must take it upon yourself to learn and practice each of them so that you can comfortably articulate trends in philanthropy, understand the different types of fundraising programs necessary for short- and long-term success, and ensure adequate organizational focus on each of the five phases of the fundraising cycle.

Budgeting and Finance

As with each of the previous four leadership elements, budgeting and finance is a fundamental component to your ability to manage an organization and assure it remains a viable and **profitable** entity. Despite having the misnomer "nonprofit" attached, good nonprofit organizations must have all of the same financial systems in place as any for-profit organization would expect, with careful attention to all forms of revenue generation, expense tracking, investment opportunities, and long-range planning to oversee capital improvements, human resources, and contractual relationships with vendors, partners, and other affiliates.

As with the first four leadership elements in this section, this overview should only serve as a reminder of the leadership topics

> Good nonprofit organizations must have all of the same financial systems in place as any for-profit organization would expect.

you should learn more about and ensure a firm understanding of so that you can articulate an approach to members of your team, your board, and ultimately a search committee. As with fundraising, you will likely be hiring or managing a professional and/or contracted resource such as an in-house CFO or contracted CPA or accounting firm. The point is that you yourself need not be certified in the area of budgeting and finance, but you must be proficient enough to understand the implications of the numbers and be able to make strategic decisions based on the financial advice you receive from your counsel. As with the previous four leadership elements, I offer these additional topical areas about which you should evaluate your knowledge and comfort level in your current organization and then apply them to your analysis of a new organization with which you might want to lead:

- **Revenue streams**. What are the primary sources of revenue for the nonprofit, and how diversified are they? Just as you would evaluate any investment portfolio, so you must ask yourself whether the organization is heavily dependent on a single revenue stream or whether it is diversified. Ideally, the organization has both earned and contributed revenue, and as discussed in the previous section, the revenues come from a mixture of individual, corporate, foundation, and potentially special-event sources. Other sources may include governmental grants and contracts and, potentially, fees for series. If the organization has funds invested in an endowment, this may also generate income that supports the operations of the nonprofit. Careful consideration and analysis must be made about each of these sources, regarding both their reliability over the past five years and their vulnerability as a revenue source going forward. How vulnerable is your organization if any one of these revenue sources were to disappear?

- **Key expenses**. As you evaluate an organization's budget and financial patterns, its expenses will be next in your analysis after you review its sources of revenue. As a nonprofit, you would expect the majority of expenses to go toward mission-based programming and the human resources necessary to provide those programs. It is difficult to put an exact percentage on what non-program-specific expenses should be (a.k.a. overhead expenses) because the nature of nonprofit programming varies widely, as does the variation about where the organization is in its life cycle. These factors significantly impact overhead expenses. For example, a start-up organization must invest a large portion of its expense budget in overhead and infrastructure, whereas an established nonprofit might have completed those investments years ago. The point is, you must understand the nature of the nonprofit's expenses and where the nonprofit is in its life cycle: start-up, rapid growth, mature, or alliance seeking, etc.

- **Capital needs**. In your evaluation of an organization's financial profile, immediately assess the current and future capital expenditures. Consider these factors: Does the nonprofit have adequate space and facility access to conduct its programs? Is this space owned or leased? What are the current and future expenses anticipated for capital improvements and deferred maintenance? Is adequate space a barrier to current programming and potential growth? All of these questions related to capital should be carefully considered in your current nonprofit and certainly scrutinized if you are considering moving into a new organization's leadership position. This is an area in which a new leader can become quickly vulnerable if the feasibility of capital growth and expansion has not been sufficient. In other words, beware of unrealistic expectations of a capital campaign being tied to the momentum of a new leader's arrival.

- **Investment Policy.** You must also give careful consideration to a nonprofit organization's short- and long-term investment and reserve policies. First and foremost, verify whether they have a written policy in place for both elements of financial health. In short, the investment policy should be at a market-appropriate level that assures that interest income used for operations does not invade the corpus of the endowed fund. That ensures the long-term health of the organization and honors donor intentions in such cases where they designated their gift to be maintained in perpetuity. Secondly, verify that the organization maintains a cash reserve that could operate the organization for three to six months. This reserve amount varies but could be evaluated by comparing with other organizations of a similar size and scope. The point is, you want to see attention paid to both of these measures of financial health for a nonprofit, and you want to be ready if either of these topics arises in an interview setting.

Your self-assessment of these skills and experiences will determine how deeply you need to dive into accounting and finance. To ensure that you are adequately prepared to provide the leadership and oversight necessary to lead an organization, you must understand whether it has adequate and diverse revenues, be able to evaluate direct and indirect expenses in support of the organization's mission, determine whether long-term analyses of capital needs and growth potential are in place, and, finally, ensure that policies are in place to protect invested assets and assure short-term viability through adequate reserves.

Armed with knowledge and experience in each of these five fundamental leadership areas, you will be well on your way to being a competitive candidate for your most ambitious nonprofit leadership opportunities. Like every other lesson you have learned on the path, know that these five areas represent a commitment to lifelong learning, and you can always learn more to enhance your leadership in strategic planning, board development, staff development, fundraising, and finance.

In the next chapter, we review all seven of the core elements discussed in this book so you can create an actionable plan going forward.

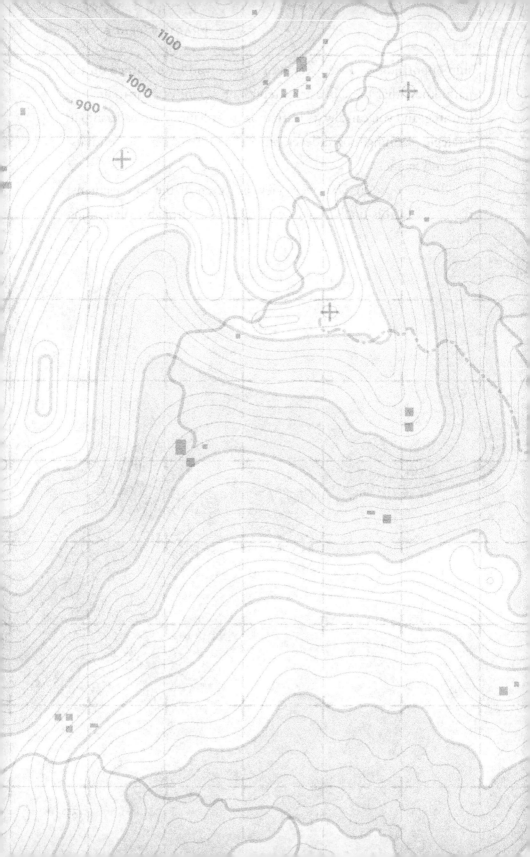

CHAPTER 9

Resources and Next Steps

B y this point in the book, you should have a good grasp of each of the seven elements that are part of the journey on the path to nonprofit leadership. Of course, none of these stops on the path is a "check it off the list and you are done" kind of accomplishment. Each represents an ongoing area of focus that should always be part of your professional development plan. Similar to the discipline required to maintain your vehicle for long-lasting life, the seven elements on the path are required maintenance and will assure that your career travels take you where you want to go.

While the previous chapters were intended to give you a clear sense of the importance of the topic in your effort to obtain a senior leadership role in the nonprofit sector, this chapter allows you to step back and see how these elements intersect and work together to accelerate your journey on the path. Here, I review each of the seven elements that you have learned so far and suggest practical applications and next steps to help you activate your plan.

Seven Elements

1. SHARPEN YOUR VISION

While there are skills, knowledge, and experiences to be gained to better position yourself for professional success, everything starts with having a clear idea of what your ultimate leadership position will be. It is okay if you are not absolutely certain about your final leadership destination; simply start by completing as much of the vision framework as possible and answering as many of the core questions as you are able:

- Where are you willing to work?

- In what nonprofit sector do you want to work?

- What kind of organizational size, scope, and culture is important to you?

- What key education, certification, and professional development do you need?

- What financial and family considerations will impact your career decisions?

In all likelihood, you have a good idea about most, if not all, of these strategic questions. But if some part of your vision framework is still to be determined, then that becomes a focal point of your ongoing professional reflection and a good starting point for conversations with colleagues, coaches, and others on the path a few years ahead of you.

2. MAP YOUR COURSE

With greater clarity around your vision framework, you can begin to fashion a plan for professional development that will build on those areas that are clear and help you to evaluate those that need additional clarity.

The first step is a self-assessment of your professional strengths and weaknesses that will provide a baseline on which your plan can be built. Utilizing the Ten Skills Worksheet (found on my website, www.pattonmcdowell.com), evaluate your current competence and confidence for each of these elements:

- *Learning Plan.* Do you have a clear sense of the skills you need to learn in the next twelve months? This plan should prioritize three elements from the assessment that most need your attention and identify specific resources, activities, and mentors associated with each. You should have a specific action item to be accomplished in the next thirty days. If you do not have a defined action item on your calendar, the plan will not activate.

- *Personal Organization.* What systems will you put in place to manage the volume of content, tasks, and activities in front of you? Being busy does not equal being productive, and success in this area includes daily, weekly, monthly, and quarterly prioritization routines to ensure that nothing falls through the cracks.

- *Leadership.* How do you practice leadership in your current position? Regardless of your place on the organizational chart, you have the ability to demonstrate leadership skills. If your current position does *not* allow the level of management necessary for advancement, then how can you assert yourself in constructive ways that will benefit your organization as well as give you the experience you need?

- *Networking.* Strategic networking will be essential for identifying new opportunities along your path to nonprofit leadership, but it will also allow you to maintain a position of authority once you assume your ultimate leadership position. Who are those comparison peers who are in a similar position to you, and who are those aspirational peers who can help you evaluate opportunities ahead?

- *Nonprofit/Sector Knowledge*. Your learning plan should certainly include content areas on which you should focus your study. What are the key issues that leaders in your nonprofit sector are discussing (ask them!), and how confident are you engaging in conversations about those topics?

- *Speaking*. All forms of communication will be critical to your nonprofit leadership—and perhaps no skill induces more stress than public speaking. Find ways to practice your public speaking in formal and informal settings and seek feedback to sharpen your preparation and delivery.

- *Writing*. Make sure that you assess the different types of written communication as you evaluate your overall writing proficiency. A senior leadership role in the nonprofit sector will require different forms of written content creation. You must be able to comfortably create a business memo that summarizes cogent information for a board committee in a concise manner, write a case for support for your organization that would convince a donor to support your cause financially, and craft a sincere handwritten note to thank a donor for their generosity. Learn to write. It is essential.

- *Listening/Conversation*. Perhaps no skill requires a more unbiased outside review than this one. Do you engage in active listening skills that assure the person you are speaking with that they have your undivided attention? Do you interrupt in conversations, meetings, or social settings? Are you thoughtful about the topics and questions you raise in a conversation, those that demonstrate both your knowledge and your understanding of the situation?

- *Financial Acumen.* For many nonprofit professionals, entry into the field comes through the programmatic side of marketing, special events, or fund development. While all of these areas are important to nonprofit leadership, ultimately, your oversight of the budget and financial health of the nonprofit will be the deciding factor in your achieving and maintaining an executive role. Nonprofits are complex businesses and often combine earned and contributed revenue streams in addition to all of the expenses inherent in the operations of programs services. What can you do to deepen your understanding of your nonprofit's financial model?

- *Strategic Planning.* While your immediate nonprofit leadership objectives will be to manage the current operation, the organization will ultimately rely on your ability to guide the long-term strategic plan. This necessitates your understanding of the strategic planning process, starting with a visioning exercise to creatively and ambitiously determine an aspirational plan to build on the current mission, but also to assess new growth potential and collaborative opportunities. How can your organization get better, dramatically better? How can your organization serve more of the people it wants to serve, or accomplish more of what it currently accomplishes, *dramatically* more? This kind of thinking is the visioning skill required for nonprofit leadership.

  While providing an aspirational and inspirational vision is the first part of your strategic planning skillset, you must also have the ability to lead an effective assessment of the organization's current state. What are the challenges that must be addressed first? What opportunities show the greatest promise for dramatic mission achievement? What threats must be contemplated, and for which contingency plans must be built?

After evaluating the organization with assessment criteria such as these, your final phase of strategic planning is effective implementation. Based on the assessment questions, what goals emerge? For each goal, what is a reasonable timeline to achieve it? What specific tasks are required to achieve the goal? What resources are necessary to achieve the goal—specifically, who is responsible for overseeing the tasks that make up the goal's implementation? Together, these strategic planning principles (vision, evaluation, and implementation) become valuable tools in your toolkit to discuss a potential leadership role as well as to actually manage the process once you arrive.

> Together, these strategic planning principles (vision, evaluation, and implementation) become valuable tools in your toolkit to discuss a potential leadership role as well as to actually manage the process once you arrive.

Once you have completed your self-assessment of each of these Ten Essential Skills and Experiences for nonprofit leadership, use the personal SWOT analysis grid to organize your thoughts around particular elements on which you want to focus: the ten are strengths on which you can build, and the one or two professional weaknesses that require your prioritized attention. What opportunities are on the horizon at your organization or within your sector and community? Are there any threats or professional risks for which you must prepare?

3. GET IN SHAPE

While the implication of this chapter does include the importance of personal fitness considerations, such as diet, sleep, and exercise, "getting in shape" also suggests a thorough review of your productivity systems and rituals. Successful nonprofit leaders must become adept at sorting through the clutter of material that exists and reducing the volume of content that can distract and diminish leadership productivity. By proactively reducing the volume of paper and digital inputs on a weekly basis, your organizational rituals can more effectively focus on prioritizing the tasks that are essential for success.

Getting in shape as a successful leader also requires a more proactive approach to your most valuable asset—your time. Proactively identify important calendar events and milestones thirty, sixty, and ninety days in advance. Do not fall victim to your calendar, having it simply fill up without your conscious oversight. A proactive mindset will prompt you to aggressively cull unnecessary events from your calendar and look for ways to diminish the time committed to routine events and meetings (is thirty minutes sufficient rather than an hour?) and the intentional calendaring of individual planning, reading, and thinking time. As a nonprofit leader, you no longer have the luxury of just attending meetings—you must be ready to lead them.

Finally, getting in shape requires a thorough review and

> Getting in shape as a successful leader also requires a more proactive approach to your most valuable asset—your time.

possible amplification of your daily, weekly, and annual routines and rituals. Preparation at every level is key. This begins with an evening ritual that reviews unfinished business from the day and prioritizes the most important strategic goals for the following day. Each morning, review every calendar item and confirm that you have what you need for each and are prepared accordingly. While the evening and morning rituals keep the leadership motor running, the weekly ritual might be the most important to assure long-term strategic success. This weekly review allows for a careful review of the previous week to evaluate any next steps and follow-up activities necessary and, as is often the case, what meetings, milestones, or deadlines you should mark in your calendar as a result. The weekly review should also provide a careful preview of the week ahead, not just what is literally on the calendar but also the preparation required for each meeting. Finally, the weekly review should consider actual tasks that must be accomplished and exactly when they will be scheduled to be accomplished.

With daily and weekly rituals in place, your chances of getting in shape increase dramatically. The final component is the use of annual personal reviews that are evaluated each quarter. Daily and weekly routines will ensure efficient productivity and task management, but quarterly reviews allow for aspirational thinking and a chance to mark progress toward long-term leadership goals. It is one thing to consider the importance of health and wellness goals, for example, but the quarterly review should document specific activities that determine progress in building strengths and eliminating weaknesses.

4. CURATE KNOWLEDGE

After you have assessed and improved all of your current leadership skills, your drive to the top of the nonprofit ladder will be fueled by your ability to identify and learn critical information. Given that new information will emerge unceasingly, you must have systems in place to organize this information as it arrives and then dedicate quality time to learning and applying it.

To begin, look at positions and job descriptions that most closely resemble the type of job you hope to achieve based on your vision framework. What do these job postings tell you about the key skills, experiences, and attributes these organizations are looking for? You will likely find consistent elements required, and those elements can directly shape the type of knowledge you need to curate for your personal library, whether books or periodicals or digital content.

Once you have identified the key types of content you must gather, establish study goals around these three key topics: books read, monthly review of key newsletters and electronic publications, and specific consultation with experts in each subject area.

Having assembled the curriculum required to stay on the leading edge of your field, the final requirement of curating knowledge is to schedule the deep work that ensures that you can actually learn the material. This is what will separate you from other aspirational leaders because this type of deep work cannot be done in a tired late-night state and likely requires high-energy morning or weekend time on your calendar. It also requires a proactive outreach to those experts in each content area who can help you review what you are learning and offer practical insight as to how your learning can be applied to an actual nonprofit leadership setting.

5. EXPRESS YOURSELF

Your leadership opportunities will be strongly influenced by your ability to communicate. In addition to positioning yourself for leadership, every aspect of actually being a successful nonprofit leader will be based on your ability to communicate with others.

As discussed within the Ten Skills Assessment, the first set of communication skills you must master are those related to various forms of written communication. Perhaps the most important written communication you will compose will be those of a persuasive nature—in particular, those instances when you are making your nonprofit's case for support and appealing for financial support.

Another type of written communication is the ability to distill complex information into easy-to-digest executive summaries. This is especially helpful in orienting board members and key stakeholders about community data or issues that are important to your organization or an explanation of programmatic options that you and your team are contemplating.

A final written skill to ponder is the personal note. Often overlooked in an era of instant electronic communication, a handwritten note is a powerful tool to demonstrate genuine gratitude to a key donor or to provide an authentic morale boost to a key employee.

Assess your written communication skills. Your first objective is to distinguish the different settings in which effective spoken communication is required and then strengthen your actual delivery in those settings. Just as in written communication, your ability to speak persuasively will be a vital skill in formal settings. Certain speaking opportunities also require efficiency and synthesis of thought that translates to effective communication. Board members expect you to communicate in a clear and concise manner, defining exactly what action is required following your comments. Leadership credibility can rise and fall based on how well you manage meetings and use your verbal skills to highlight key points, accelerate an agenda if necessary, and call for a decision when the time is right.

The least tangible communication skill, but equally important to any other, is your interpersonal communication and listening ability. Are you a good active listener? Eye contact, appropriate body language, lack of interrupting, and intelligent follow-up questions all demonstrate good active listening skills. Equally important to your ability to effectively interact in those settings is adequately preparing *before* the meeting actually takes place. Your ability to communicate in an informal setting comfortably and confidently will dramatically increase if you have done your homework. This preparation will demonstrate your attention to detail and make your interpersonal communication even more effective.

6. BUILD COMMUNITY

To distinguish yourself as a nonprofit leader, much depends on your intrinsic motivation and the discipline necessary to tackle each of the elements described in this book as part of the path to nonprofit leadership. However, the most effective current and aspiring nonprofit leaders maximize the resources within their community and actively pursue other resources that can help them on their journey.

The first exercise is to identify two like-minded colleagues who are in a similar position to yours but at a different organization. Utilize them in a mutually beneficial way by comparing self-assessments and discussing resources that might help address areas of weakness. Similarly, identify two aspirational colleagues who are further along on their leadership journey, perhaps in an executive role similar to the one you hope to achieve. These four strategic relationships can do much to build community and accelerate your journey on the path.

Look for other targeted outreach that might help you to address certain questions or advise you about a particular challenge you are facing. Perhaps your goal could be to interview three senior development directors about their experience running a capital campaign if that is something on the horizon for you. You might interview three board members who have gone through a nonprofit merger and see what lessons they have learned as a result.

Finally, the strategic networking described here will help you to build a framework for your personal board of directors. Just as your nonprofit organization depends on a diverse and talented board of directors to help it strategically succeed, so your professional journey will benefit from a similarly talented group of individuals who can help you to address current areas of need as identified through your self-assessment exercises, but also help you to look ahead on the path and prepare you for those nonprofit leadership opportunities that will come your way.

The makeup of your personal board of directors should be similar to your nonprofit board. You want a diverse set of professional skills that can address any of the strategic functions you will need for nonprofit leadership: fundraising, finance, strategic planning, and board governance, to name a few. You can also focus on topical expertise within the sector you hope to serve as a CEO, and you might also recruit experience in other communities if you are contemplating working in other markets than the one you are in now.

7. PRACTICE LEADERSHIP

While the path to nonprofit leadership is all about preparing you for your ultimate executive position, you can certainly begin practicing key leadership skills before you actually arrive at the position to which you aspire.

Leadership Programs

Direct networking and one-on-one coaching provide the highest-quality professional development and are the most efficient uses of your discretionary time, but leadership programs can certainly add value as well. These programs will afford you knowledge, allow you to network with other talented professionals within and outside your sector, and provide accountability to your progress based on attendance and other program requirements. Of course, these programs warrant a careful evaluation regarding where they fit on your path to nonprofit leadership, as there are certain time and cost factors to consider.

There are many programs of varying size, scope, and duration to consider, but I will share three types that might pique your interest.

Geographic Leadership Programs

In my home city, Leadership Charlotte is a good example of a community-based program that provides a diverse group of leaders an opportunity to increase their community knowledge, civic network, and understanding of key issues facing all sectors of the city. Like Leadership Charlotte, Leadership North Carolina attracts leaders from both for-profit and nonprofit organizations and might be representative of a program in your state or country as well. These programs provide a deeper understanding of the issues facing the public, private, and governmental sectors across a geographic range that corresponds with your nonprofit's reach. In addition to the depth of knowledge you will gain and the contacts you will add to your network, you will also expand your view of other organizations outside of your own that might become referral partners, corporate sponsors, or even future employers.

Other Leadership Programs

It is worth exploring other sources for leadership development in your community and region. Often, large community foundations host leadership programs or are indirectly involved in their implementation. Check as well with local and state-wide universities for the various leadership programs with which they may be associated, especially if you graduated from the institution yourself. Your state might also have a program like the William C. Friday Fellowship, in which I was a participant, where you learn invaluable leadership lessons and tools for collaboration and working across differences. The Center for Creative Leadership is another program based in North Carolina that offers programs for individuals and groups from across the country.

Facilitated Leadership Groups and Masterminds

You may find formal and informal leadership groups emerge through nonprofit associations like the Association of Fundraising Professionals (AFP), Certified Fundraising Executives (CFRE), or the Council for Advancement and Support of Education (CASE). I offer Mastermind small-group leadership coaching programs as well, selecting six to eight like-minded nonprofit professionals to participate in a guided cohort-style program over a three-month period. This provides a deeper dive into all of the concepts described in this book. For more information, go to www.pattonmcdowell.com/mastermind.

CONCLUSION

T
hank you for committing to the nonprofit sector and for making senior leadership your ultimate goal. Strong leaders are making a difference in all types of nonprofits, from small organizations focused on disadvantaged neighborhoods to large entities fostering global movements. These efforts, however, will not continue unless more motivated individuals like you take it upon themselves to embrace leadership. I hope you will revisit each of the seven "stops" along the path to nonprofit leadership often and that the tools provided in this book will help not only you but also others in your organization as you pass along the gift of nonprofit leadership to them.

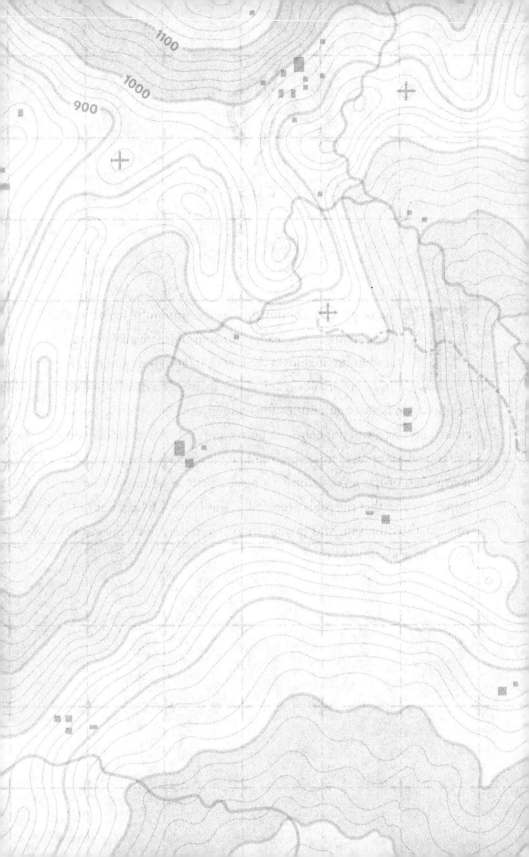

ABOUT THE AUTHOR

Patton McDowell has enjoyed a successful thirty-year career in nonprofit leadership, strategic planning, and organizational development. His consulting practice, PMA Consulting, has allowed him to work with more than 250 organizations, including nonprofits focused on healthcare, education, arts and culture, and human services. Prior to founding PMA Consulting in 2009, he served as the vice president for university advancement at Queens University of Charlotte after serving as the vice chancellor for university advancement at UNC Wilmington. A native of Elizabeth City, North Carolina, Patton received a BA in education from UNC Chapel Hill, where he was a Morehead Scholar, an MBA from the McColl School of Business at Queens, and his Doctorate in Education (Organizational Change and Leadership) from the University of Southern California. He is a Certified Fundraising Executive (CFRE), a Master Trainer for AFP International, and the host of the weekly podcast *Your Path to Nonprofit Leadership*.

Thank you for reading
Your Path To Nonprofit Leadership.

If you enjoyed this book and found it helpful
on your path, please consider visiting the
site where you purchased it and write a brief
review.

To learn more about our programs or
to subscribe to our newsletter,
please visit www.pattonmcdowell.com.

CPSIA information can be obtained
at www.ICGtesting.com
Printed in the USA
JSHW071720191222
35156JS00006B/151